BÔ YIN RÂ

(JOSEPH ANTON SCHNEIDERFRANKEN)

VOLUME 18
OF THE 32-VOLUME CYCLE

THE GATED GARDEN

MORE LIGHT

For more information
about the books of Bô Yin Râ and
titles available in English translation
visit The Kober Press web site at
www.kober.com

THE KOBER PRESS PUBLISHES THE ONLY ENGLISH TRANSLATIONS
OF THE BOOKS OF BÔ YIN RÂ AUTHORIZED BY THE KOBER VERLAG,
SWITZERLAND. THE KOBER VERLAG PUBLISHES THE BOOKS OF
BÔ YIN RÂ IN THE ORIGINAL GERMAN AND HAS PROTECTED
THEIR INTEGRITY SINCE THE AUTHOR'S LIFETIME.

BÔ YIN RÂ
(JOSEPH ANTON
SCHNEIDERFRANKEN)

MORE LIGHT

TRANSLATED FROM THE GERMAN BY
JAN SCHYMURA, MALKA WEITMAN
AND ERIC STRAUSS

THE
KOBER
PRESS

BERKELEY, CALIFORNIA

CONTENTS

PREFACE

THIS BOOK ORIGINATED FROM ESSAYS that were originally published separately and then collected together in book form in 1921 under the present title. This edition was published in 1936 and incorporates changes that clarify certain passages.

At this time, with the book *The Gated Garden (Hortus Conclusus)*, I have completed the thirty-two books that comprise my spiritual teaching cycle. I have designated the title of that book to also be the name of the entire teaching cycle, as the metaphor of a gated garden symbolically expresses the essential quality of my works and the attitude necessary to approach their inner meaning.

The legacy I leave behind in these thirty-two volumes is an organically linked gift of teaching and should be taken as a unified whole.

This teaching cycle would be viewed in the wrong light if one were to regard it as simply a literary production: it is not just something that I have created; it is not a result of the urge to create that is familiar to human beings. Even if this teaching cycle had not been written down—even if I had not given it form in words—its contents would still be identical with myself: it is one with my eternal being that is the source of my life.

Until my day, there have not been among all the peoples on this earth as many as ten human beings in existence in the realm of time who were able to embed in words their own eternal being and unite this with the capacity of mortals to feel within. Those who had this ability could truly say: "Heaven and earth shall pass away, but my words will not pass away." (Matthew 24:35 KJV)

The forewords and afterwords of my texts of guidance are as much a part of these words as the texts themselves, and should therefore not be regarded as separate from the body of texts they enclose.

Just like precious stones which have long ago taken on what was thought to be their final shape are sometimes cut anew so that they may reflect still more light, the content of this book has also been "cut" anew. No one who is familiar with the previous version will doubt that the new treatment, carefully reworked to bring even greater value to the original intent, has given its crystalline content even more luster. This is especially true of the chapters I have retitled for the sake of clarity. I therefore include only this new version in my now completed cycle of books.

Like a team of horses reluctantly pulling a wagon, many of my words have been put into service in places where they were not at all comfortable being "harnessed." Thus, I have been forced to take steps to protect them from future misinterpretation and misuse. Such protection, heaven knows, should be unnecessary because I have never left the slightest doubt that I do not serve any human institution, nor do I follow any human ideology. Each of the thirty-two books comprising my spiritual guidance has been dedicated by the Eternal for one purpose: to form for my spiritual body a physical "body" made of words, so that through the words I could be perceived by others.

Even if in centuries to come the life of my spirit shall become the personal possession of countless individuals through their own spiritual efforts, it will nevertheless belong to each one as an undiminished whole: Its substance will be fused with their own eternal spiritual substance.

જી

WORDS OF
GUIDANCE

THERE ARE TIMES IN THE HISTORY OF humankind in which the human beings of this earth feel utterly estranged from their spiritual homeland, no longer even capable of believing that this homeland may exist.

There are other times, however, in which many seekers turn towards the Spirit once again. They sense that human beings of this earth can reclaim the spiritual heritage that is theirs, even though they may no longer know the path that leads them there. And so they search in darkness—blindly trusting every path that seems to them mysterious and strange.

For this reason it has become necessary to introduce more light into the confusing darkness, where countless seekers wander aimlessly in labyrinths of spiritual theories and speculation or follow spiritual "teachers" who lead them only to the veneration of their supposed guides' own persons and their folly.

⚮

WE ARE NOW IN THE MIDST of such a period of spiritual seeking, even though many human beings are still ruled by their crude animal nature and are reaping the rewards of its greedy, self-serving triumphs.

It would be irresponsible to assert that today's seekers—who are striving towards the light of the Spirit despite all the currents that pull them in the opposite direction—are motivated only by sensationalism, idle curiosity and a vain desire to flaunt their intellectual superiority.

It would be foolish to look down upon those seekers who search ancient religions, hoping to find the common thread that will guide them out of the dark labyrinths of philosophical speculation and lead them to the light of true knowledge.

There are many ways to escape the darkness and those who have been able to do so should remain faithful to the way that has led them to the Light and not wonder if other ways also exist.

Among today's seekers there are many who have grown weary of searching because each path they entered upon only led them astray and each "shepherd" they blindly trusted proved to be as ignorant of the way to the Spirit as the flock they were leading.

I write for all such seeking souls. I write as one who speaks of things with which he is familiar, out of a fullness of experience that is seldom possible for mortals. Those other seekers, however, who believe they have already found what they had sought are here presented with a touchstone that separates the real from the illusory.

୬

THE VARIOUS CHAPTERS of this book developed separately and may thus be read at will.

Each chapter was written in order to answer the questions of numerous inquirers as I had not time and energy to deal with each person's questions separately. The topics I cover were determined by the kinds of questions put to me. Thus, I mention things I would not have thought to write about had it not been for the reasonable request of the inquirer. Also, repetitions to accommodate the nature of the requests I received became unavoidable.

All chapters are spiritually linked—it could not be otherwise—and, taken together, form a firm foundation upon which readers, each in their own way, may safely build.

There will scarcely be any reader who will not benefit greatly from this book and to whom it would not truly bring more Light. All those longing for true insight should realize, however, that real insights into the mysteries of the eternal life of the Spirit cannot be attained by pursuing yet another religion or philosophical doctrine. For this reason, those who search for truth in my writings will not encounter any articles of faith or a system of beliefs that must be accepted without question.

Instead, I show searching individuals diverse vistas of the Spirit towards which they are striving, using ever new imagery, trusting in their ability to feel and sense and calling on them to use their own judgment. My intention is to give them a way, through these varied texts, to reach an inner certainty for *them-selves*—a certainty that every soul may attain only through its *own* experience. I have not the slightest interest in having readers agree with what they read in my writings through the use of their intellect. I simply want to help them reach the inner state which alone reveals what the darkness all around conceals from their soul.

It would be totally wrong to try to discover credos or articles of faith in my teaching cycle—that is, dogma that must be accepted in a formulaic manner. One will only be able to immerse one's self in these teachings, brought by me into this realm of time, if one allows each individual passage of these texts to have an effect upon one's *soul* by first seeking *to sense my timeless Being* in it. Once one is able to feel this, one will also inwardly receive from out of my eternal, true Being every "answer" desired and, at the same time, the certainty of their irrefutable truth as testimony of timeless Reality.

It would also be wrong to think that one could arrive at greater insights than can be gained from the written teachings that I have composed by discussing them with me personally.

Those who speak with me encounter my mortal, physical body—not my eternal, spiritual *self*—since they lack the spiritual sense organs needed for such perception. To be sure, in a face-to-face meeting I can give answers using the vehicle of my temporal, physical brain, but it is impossible to formulate language, while in someone's presence, that can transmit my *spiritual* Being such that my substance can penetrate that person's own inner being.

Solitude, absolute isolation from the vibratory energy of other brains, and a state of almost inconceivably intense concentration are necessary for the creation of such language.

❧

CHAPTER ONE

TO ALL THOSE TIRED OF SLEEPING

A CALL TO AWAKEN

OUR DAYS ARE FILLED WITH SIGNS AND wonders and the Spirit sweeps across the surface of the earth like a windstorm, but the humans of this earth lie fast asleep and cannot be roused from their slumber.

Spellbound by their dream-state, they seek for wonders in the world around them but cannot find the wonders of Reality.

They seek for signs of light but can only penetrate the realm of darkness. Lost in their dream-state, they would be overcome by fear and fright if Light could truly reach them.

And some, while babbling in their sleep, claim their cherished faith is supported by science, while others believe they have overcome all need for faith by virtue of the knowledge they have acquired.

None suspect that immutable Reality is independent of their dreams and has no need of mental knowledge or belief in order to bring forth signs and wonders.

None suspect that signs and wonders surround them even while they toss and turn restlessly and wildly in their sleep, seeking something that they cannot find there.

❧

HAD THERE NOT in every epoch been at least a few who forcefully wrested themselves from their slumber, then also for the others no awakening would be possible. Lost in their sleep-state, they would vanish from the embrace of the All-Conscious, like a fleeting night-time dream that disappears upon arising.

But the Princes of the Light found at least a few awakened eyes and ears to whom they could make plain the signs of Light; to whom they could proclaim the *Word* of Light. These awakened few are the *only* ones who can rouse you from your slumber if you are willing— even now in this, your time on earth—unless your innermost has died already and this death has wrapped your being in its leaden shroud.

℘

WHOEVER READS these words, even if you are still spellbound by your dream-state: search the deepest recesses of your being for traces of the memory of something you had once possessed. And there perhaps, in the hazy half-light, you will discover a precious gem that reminds you of the treasure house that once was yours.

But those who are so mired in slumber that they can no longer find within even a faint remembrance of a life before this life on earth in which they were awake—let them not read my words. Without the power to rouse these sleepers, my words will only disturb their fond, familiar dreams—the dreams they will hold dear until the day they realize that all they thought was real is nothing but delusion.

If I am to give you more than empty words, then I shall have to put an end to many a cherished dream.

If I am to rouse you from your slumber, I must not shy away from saying things that will be hard for you to hear.

If I am to awaken you to the light of *day*, I must eschew the worn-out language of those you imagine are your saviors and redeemers.

∞

I TOO WAS ONCE a dreaming pupil of these imagined saviors—although only with the physical dimension of my being. Once I had been roused from my slumber I realized that there exists only one savior, born unto us from the primordial time of the Beginning. This savior can never be found in the insipid stories and stale atmosphere of the dream-state.

Truly, voices call to you in the deserts of your present lives and the one true savior, who may be found when you have awakened to Reality, is at all times being born "immaculately" as every individuated being emerges from the Ground of Being. Yet, the roaring blasts of the conch shell,* which summon all who are called to master the most challenging of tasks, are too harsh and wild, and disturb the play-life of your dream-state.

---

* This is a reference to Triton's conch shell. Triton is a mythological Greek god who is known for blowing on a twisted conch shell to calm or raise the waters of the sea. He is the herald of his father, Poseidon, god of the sea.

And so you have transformed the tolling sounds emanating from the primordial world of the Beginning—the sounds the divine breath sends forth ever anew—into a sweet-sounding, seductive shepherd's tune, so that it may lull you back into the comfortable embrace of your dreams.

Behind each individual you call "savior" and "redeemer" stood one who truly was these things; who carried within himself the one eternal Savior and who had awakened from sleep and dreams and brought forth the "Son of Man" in his very person and honed it to perfection. Yet, your romantic notions of these sublime individuals who you now honor and praise are simply creations of your dream-state—without substance and mere shadows of reality.

❧

WHETHER YOU CONSIDER yourselves to be believers or nonbelievers, in either case you are thinking of a god you have created in your imagination—a god you venerate or a god you have decided to banish from your dreams.

You practice the most absurd sort of idolatry. You imagine that you "know" and "honor" the "one true God"—or you deny that this god exists and fashion new gods who are no less figments of your dream-state. Numbed by your dream existence, none of you suspect that your debates about the nature of god, or whether god exists at all, merely pit one empty nothing against another empty nothing.

But know this: Just as behind each individual you call Savior and Redeemer there stood one who truly was these things, so too behind all your speculation about god there exists a *Reality*—and this Reality is completely independent of your dreams.

I who today addresses you as one who is awake—I too was once caught up in your dreams of God. I once believed in this god and then denied that he existed. And then, waking to my eternal self, I realized that no dream akin to the dreams of mortal humans could comprehend the vastness and the splendor of the Living God.

With words of thunder I wish to rouse you from your sleep so that I might lead you towards the deep and silent stillness of Reality—for only here can your Living God be born within you.

ॐ

IN EACH OF YOU—in *you* and in *you*—your mortal consciousness must be prepared so that the Living God can be born within. And only when you are so prepared will you experience its presence.

You will not find the Living God within all the vastness of space nor beyond space. You will not find the Living God until it has been born within *you* and can be felt by you as real and tangible.

You blaspheme against your Living God when you believe in the god you have imagined in your dream-state, or when you deny that this imagined god exists.

You blaspheme against eternal Being—the only absolute Reality—which seeks to form itself within you as your Living God, and whose form you are, when you consider your-self to already be "the work of his hands."

❧

LIKE BIRDS DRIVEN ALOFT by the wind, your ideas about god have soared far beyond all waking reality. In your dream state you imag-ined a god that is, in truth, merely an intellec-tual fetish. The heathen carves his god from a block of wood until it speaks to his soul; you create your god in your mind, out of thoughts, and then insist that god must be as you have imagined "him" to be. And even if, in your dream state, you discover that nothing real ever issues from your idol's lips, you still refuse to relinquish your belief.

You try to grasp the unformed sea of Spirit, but it slips through your fingers even as you believe you are holding onto it. You do not realize that the living Spirit needs to form itself "in the image" of the human beings who issue forth from it, if it is to become the "god" for any human here on earth.

It has been written that: "...the Spirit searcheth all things, yea, the deep things of God." (1 Corinthians 2:10, KJV) And you, in turn, presume to search the Spirit and to penetrate its depths. You endow it with the attributes you deem desirable and, pleased with your own wisdom and unconscious of your blasphemy, you "reverently" call your own creation "God."

Those who deny this god exists are no less slaves of delusion than those who believe in him, because this denial is itself delusion.

Thoughts create idols and thoughts destroy them—without touching reality in the slightest.

∽

TRULY, THERE IS a Reality that gives rise to these dream-state delusions, but it would not truly be Reality if such delusions could affect it.

Unapproachable as a lightning bolt flashing from cloud to cloud, blinding as the sun at noon and yet also cloaked in darkness, Reality is eternally alive, eternally generating its own self in all its awesome might and vastness.

This Reality is infinitely distant from your idea of the Spirit's nature, infinitely distant from all conceptions about "God" upon which the religions of this earth are founded.

And yet, whenever a "God" answers the prayers of the faithful, whether they pray to Brahma, Allah, the Father, Lord and Savior, Christ or Buddha, it is only this Reality that responds to their prayers.

Reality manifests itself only to awakened souls.

Reality is only comprehensible to those who have left sleep and dreams behind forever.

Only those who have awakened and with waking senses can discern their God, may hope their God will speak the Word of Life within them.

As long as you hope to encounter the Godhead while still in a dream-state, you will continue to be deceived by your self-created idols and will have to endure the indignity of being their plaything.

⁂

Do NOT THINK you are powerless or that these idols hold some power you do not.

It is *you* who have endowed them with power, without even knowing you have done so.

You still are unaware that you have the ability to bestow power and that your power consists precisely in being able to command forces far mightier than yourself.

You have fashioned idols out of your thoughts and endowed them with power through your faith, which is a product of your mind.

You use science to either mock faith or support it, but you do not yet know that the reach of faith is limitless and far beyond what you believe.

The highest of your powers are bestowed upon you by faith. Through the power that flows from faith you can master mighty forces—the primal energies of the cosmos—and cause them to become your servants; your faith can liberate the awesome power that lies dormant in these energies, awaiting your command.

Through your faith you can direct these powers to serve you and, likewise, through your faith you can cause them to torment you— even to annihilate you.

Through your faith in the idols you created by your thoughts you have endowed them with much power but, truly, their power has not been a blessing for you—it has imprisoned you instead.

These days it often is said that "thoughts are things" and just as real as physical reality. But I say to you that your thoughts are *more* than the "things" of this earth. Your thoughts are energies—conscious and single-minded energies that cannot be compared to any "thing" on earth—and are suffused with a greedy will to live.

From such energies you have fashioned your idols and through your faith endowed them with the power to do you good or evil according to their will.

You say: "For whom the Lord loveth, He chasteneth." (Hebrews 12:6 KJV) And your God, created by you from the single-minded, conscious energies of your thoughts, is *forced* by you to chasten you—even to torment you—the more intensely you love the mental image from which you formed him.

∽

But the God created by billions of believers—lost in their dream state—over the ages cannot be destroyed from one day to the next even if you try to kill him by proclaiming that god is dead.

Again and again he will demonstrate to you that he is still alive, nourished by the countless believers who constantly reinvent him in their thoughts, certain of the power conferred upon him by faith that is daily renewed.

You think yourselves to be *Übermenschen* and proclaim that "God is dead";* all the while he mocks you and your self-assuredness, for his life is secured for millennia through the faith of his believers.

You will not escape his might until the day arrives that wrests you from sleep and dreams.

༜

Bᴜᴛ ᴛᴏᴅᴀʏ you are still slaves to your dreams.

You still hold fast to the dream-state which keeps you from that day and believe it to be waking life.

You are not aware that even the dreams you dream during your nights here on earth are closer to waking life than what you call the reality of day.

---

* The *Übermensch* and the death of God are concepts in the philosophy of Friedrich Nietzsche. According to Nietzsche, human beings must free themselves from reliance on looking to an other-worldly god as the source of morality and meaning. Instead, they should strive to become superior beings (*Übermenschen*) who create their own values and meaning, rooted exclusively in this earth and tailored specifically to each individual.

You love your dream-state all too much—just like a newly-hatched bird inside a cage that has pecked its way out of the egg but does not flee the cage, even though the door of its prison is wide open.

The bird feels at home in the cage because the only life it knows is behind the bars that hold it captive. Similarly, *you* only feel at home with the knowledge of things that are familiar to you.

You are afraid to flee the world of mental knowledge in which you are imprisoned and escape into the free, awake world of Reality that lies beyond all mental knowledge. It is a realm only those can experience who have awakened in themselves and thus realize their true nature, freed from the torment of the endless "need to know."

And should someone come along who lives in this world of Reality and can truly speak of it—even though he still also experiences the world of dreams in which you live—you immediately descend upon that person with a thousand questions expecting answers which you think will increase your knowledge. Rare are the individuals who will leave the quest for mental knowledge behind in the world of dreams and become *real* in the world of Reality.

&

HERE IS WHERE the key is hidden: in the deep caverns guarded by the "Mothers" since time immemorial.*

Whoever will not descend into these depths will never grasp this key.

Those who are unwilling to leave behind the knowledge gathered in their dream-state, and to consign it to the world of dreams; those who are not able to fearlessly let go of the self that they have known and to turn instead to face the unknown that can never be touched by mental knowledge—such dreaming individuals will search for eternities without finding what they seek.

---

* The realm of the mothers is an allusion to a scene in the second part of Goethe's *Faust* and is also a concept in the Greek Mysteries. The realm of the mothers can also refer to the depths of the psyche. Carl Jung describes it as being related to the creative powers of the unconscious.

25

These dreamers cherish their dreams so much that a powerful will to awaken can never grow within them.

જી

IT IS YOUR NEED TO KNOW that keeps you from true knowledge; it is your need to know that keeps you from awakening.

It is your need to know that enslaves you to your idols—whatever name you might give them.

As long as you are subjugated to a self-created idol fashioned from your driven, probing thoughts—even if it is your custom to call this idol "the one true God"—the living Spirit will not be able to form itself and be born within you as your Living God.

જી

UNTIL THE LIVING GOD has been born within you, you will remain a godless worshiper of idols in your world of dreams.

Until the Living God has been born within you, you belong to the living dead. You hardly can imagine, even in your most audacious dreams, what your *life* truly is—this life that you believe you know so well.

Until your Living God has been born within you, the "knowledge" you acquired in your dream-state will keep you on a leash and lead you where it will. Everything you now believe to be true, even truer than things you might once have believed, are merely new errors, new dreams—valid only in the world of your dreams.

Only your will to awaken can wrest you from your dreams and help those who have already awakened to rouse you from your slumber.

Only in souls who have awakened may the Living God be born "of water and of the spirit." (John 3:5 KJV) You do not need to know what these words mean—but if you would *experience* their meaning, you must first awaken within.

ॐ

TODAY YOU MERELY *wish* to awaken yet *want* to continue dreaming your dreams.

You are still bound by the world of dreams that has held you captive from your earliest years.

You are still bound by the dreams of others and dare not venture out on your own path. You dread the solitude through which you will have to travel tirelessly if you would one day reach the new companions who await you in the world of Reality.

And yet, you must overcome these obstacles if you would ever attain the lucid clarity of waking day.

I earnestly advise you—*today*, even as you read these words: Summon your resolve and commit to no longer surrendering to the collective sleep and dreams of those around you.

I earnestly advise you—*today*, with steadfast will: Dedicate your energies to understanding, in the light of my teachings, that although you think you are awake, you are indeed asleep and dreaming.

I earnestly advise you to relinquish all of your present knowledge and, with perfect ease of mind, consign it to the world of dreams from whence you gathered it. Insofar as you are still connected with others who reside in the world of dreams you should, without a qualm, continue to make use of it—but do not expect that *they* can answer those last questions that move the human heart.

❧

LASTLY I ADVISE YOU to mistrust all popular religions, so satisfied with their self-invented pious phrases, that still can influence you in your dream-state—especially if they try to win you over by making use of fear. And mistrust even more those who attempt to found a new religion or spiritual movement by mixing together all the beliefs that dreamers have fashioned.

Mistrust all those who try to reinvent the old faith of their dream-state and paint it over with some supposed "science."

Wrest yourself away from the ideas that other dreamers planted in your dreams in answer to your questions about life's final matters.

To be sure, one may find a grain of truth in every dream-state faith just as some actual bodily sensation or occurrence in the outer world may find its way into a dream you dream at night. But it is precisely because truth can be mixed in with delusion that you can be so easily misled; the few grains of truth in the faith you now follow can lead you to believe in the truth of all the rest—and thus be your undoing.

The Truth of the light-filled Reality—that truth you are now striving to reach—cannot be discovered through reason or the laws of logic.

What you now wish to attain is above all thought and only after having attained it may you elevate your thoughts and reflect upon it.

What you now wish to attain you must *become*. The methods you have used before to grasp the truth cannot reveal it to you.

❧

YOUR FIRST EFFORTS should be focused on creating a spaciousness within, a vast emptiness within you, so that something new may enter and fill your being.

Do not expect that this change can happen overnight.

Depending on your individual nature, it may take years, decades, or even longer until you are ready to be safely roused from your slumber.

Courage and perseverance must be your guides as you begin your journey.

If you earnestly try to escape the fetters of your dream-state and the dream-world you have shared with others, then your perceptions will gradually change. The things you think you know will appear in a different light, and this change will confirm to you that you are on the right path.

But do not believe that miracles, which in the world of dreams are seen as signs of awakening, will now begin to happen to you.

Signs and miracles *will* occur on your new path but I doubt you will notice them until the "third eye" has opened on your forehead.

But it is not necessary that you notice them now.

Many have been close to awakening only to fall back into slumber and dreams because they were not yet prepared to cope with the mysterious weaving of wonders they encountered on their path and, instead, let themselves be anesthetized by overpowering, seductive influences.

℘

THE MORE SOBER and free of romanticism you can be, the better able you will be to tread your path.

Do not expect or strive for anything other than this: to awaken from your slumber and the world of dreams you share with others.

The more this one striving animates your being, the more strongly you can focus on your goal, maintaining all the while an unswerving inner calm—the more you may hope that help can reach you. Indeed, you *must* have help along this path; without it you never could perfect your inner work, no matter how great your achievements in this earthly world of dreams.

⊗

DO NOT THINK IT UNJUST if you are able to attain that which others still cannot.

I speak to you as one who *can* come close to awakening at this time, even though you see around you only those oppressed by fear-filled dreams. If, however, you are one who is not yet able to awaken, then my words, in any case, will not be understood by you and likely will not be understood by you for some time. You will not hear a similar call to awaken until a later time—perhaps only when millennia have passed and you are in a different form of being—and you will then be ready to recognize the call and follow it.

≈

THE "DIVINE JUSTICE" that people seek—yet do not find—in this earthly existence is merely a demand from those still living in a dream-state.

In the world of Reality, however—which surrounds us yet cannot be perceived by those who seek it in their dream-state—true justice reigns, undisputed and secure. But you will only be able to perceive it once *you* have become real within this world of Reality.

Only then will you understand that the "divine justice" you now demand would be *unjust* were it come to pass as you imagine.

And much of what today appears to you as glaringly unjust in the way the world is ordered will then be revealed to you as just beyond all question. For the effects of our deeds and impulses begin to manifest in the phantom realms by the shore of the spiritual world even before the death of the physical body—these final and most implacable consequences of earth-born impulses.

Do not seek to glimpse in advance what can only be your rightful possession after having paid the price for it through unceasing, faithful devotion to the path.

Any fulfillment in the world of Reality can only be granted you after you have complied with the clear and precisely defined laws of that world.

Nothing here can be evaded or bargained down in price.

Those who would help you obtain what you desire by fraudulent means are the most deplorable of your enemies, far more cruel than any *honest* enemy you may encounter on the straight path you travel.

Do not trust a single word of those who promise you fast results without strict discipline.

Do not trust any teacher who would guide you towards becoming a seer of spirits using methods derived from the world of dreams.

Do not trust the words you may hear from the mouths of somnambulists and mediums during trance states, which are simply crises of their nervous system.

Do not trust any teaching that makes the highest birthright and most sublime goal of every human being dependent on a particular diet or on fakir-like "exercises."

All these things will only lead you to new dreams, submerging you more deeply still in the sleep-state you are wanting to escape.

※

THOSE WHO TRULY WISH to awaken must believe in themselves.

Let those who earnestly desire to enter the world of Reality as "resurrected" beings test the truth of my words, each alone in their own heart, and then live their lives in accordance with my teachings.

In this way they shall become masters of their destiny in the realm of Eternity.

The gates of the temples of timeless wisdom will open to them—gates which have heretofore been closed because only those who have awakened within can find the keys to unlock them.

Spiritual helpers will always be near, as often as their help is needed.

They will be there to help the seeking soul awaken to the Spirit; this awakening will shape the soul so that it may receive the form that will endure for all Eternity.

It makes no sense and is useless, however, to expect that spiritual help will be given where one's own energies suffice. These innate energies want to be *used*, so that they may unfold through action.

Those who have grown tired of sleeping and have summoned their own energies in the service of awakening will more easily reach their sublime goal.

CHAPTER TWO

THE
MASTER BUILDERS
OF HUMANITY'S
ETERNAL TEMPLE

THERE IS A SMALL COMMUNITY OF MEN ON this planet who are united in a purely spiritual way—bound together by a covenant consecrated within the realm of Eternity. Their silent work has gone on for millennia, hidden from human eyes, without use of spoken or written words, for they work in *spiritual* ways. They are able to reach all human beings whose souls, through their own inner work, have become ready to receive the rays of spiritual light that emanate from this hidden community—and this light will then fill their hearts.

To the Western mind such a thing may sound incredible and be regarded with skepticism. Asians, however, live in a region which is closer to the geophysically determined place where the metaphysical force field of this spiritual community is concentrated, and would sooner doubt the existence of the sun than to doubt what every aware individual there understands about the workings of this hidden, silent community—and which more than a few individuals have also experienced.

But even in the West, there were those who knew and cloaked with silence such inner knowledge of spiritual Reality, already since the days of the *Edda*.* The Middle Ages of the Occident were filled with inspiring tidings emanating from a noble circle of enlightened beings—individuals who were unified with their own Living God—even if this knowledge was not everywhere as clearly brought to light as in the legend of the Holy Grail and its noble knights. Traces of these tidings can still be found in legends, folk beliefs and poetry.

In more recent times, circles of explorers of the mystical traditions knew of the existence of the Wise Men of the East. For half a century so-called "theosophical" books have been speaking of "mahatmas" and their

---

* *Edda* is a Norse term referring to two literary works written down in Iceland during the 13th century, but containing material from earlier sources, reaching back into the Viking Age.

brotherhood—also referred to as "The White Lodge."* But the beings who go by these names are not at all like those explorers believe them to be, or the way they are described in those books. They do not constitute a Masonic lodge or similar circle nor some sort of secret society. Rather, they are a purely *spiritual* community that cannot be compared to any other association of human beings on this earth.

But because of these "theosophical" publications, the members of this spiritual community came to be thought of as possessing mysterious powers—a reputation that they never intended for themselves and one which they regard as mere caricature and worthy of contempt.

In these writings they have been portrayed as sorcerers or demigods possessed with extraordinary scientific knowledge—a type of knowledge to which they are, in fact, quite indifferent. They have been endowed with godlike omniscience about matters of this earth and power over spirit and matter virtually unlimited in scope.

---

* The Theosophical Society was founded in 1875. This book was first published in 1921.

These ideas made sense to many of the Theosophists because, in the early days of the movement, they witnessed strange phenomena—strange enough for the uninformed to ascribe them to the workings of demigods. Thus arose the belief that the originators of such happenings and the Wise Men of the East were identical—and that these wise men were possessed of super powers. The Theosophists then introduced the idea that mahatmas are supermen and spread this idea throughout the Western world.

The true mahatmas—if one would persist in using this over-used and worn-out Indian honorific to refer to the circle of those who are illuminated by eternal Light and incarnated in mortal bodies here on earth—have never fathered "spiritual movements" or tried to found associations by seeking to impress humans through the use of fakir arts and professed scientific omniscience.

They regard the compulsive drive of Western science to find out every "why" and "wherefore" as a kind of spiritual vivisection and regard the thirst for knowledge to be appropriate only when it confines itself to exploration of normal human experience within this material world—and does not try to reach beyond those boundaries.

Their spiritual knowledge is of a different kind: It is a certainty of soul with regard to spiritual matters and has not the least to do with scientific scholarship.

Nevertheless, they consider it desirable for the members of their spiritual community, during their life on earth, to have an understanding of the matters of this world. In other words, it is expected that they acquire at least the minimum level of education typical of individuals at the time and in the culture where they live. But in accordance with spiritual law, it is also true that any shepherd, unable even to write his own name and having grown up far from all cultural centers, could become one of them—provided that he is *born* to this calling. No one can be trained to be a master any more than a person without talent can be trained to be an artistic genius.

It remains only to point out that a master of this sublime circle is a real mahatma in the true sense of this word—meaning "great soul." A mahatma can be born anywhere on earth—not only in India, China, or Tibet. Further, it

is of no consequence whether he comes into
direct contact with the spiritual source and
center of the Brotherhood on Earth early or
late in life or whether he passes through the
spirals of spiritual schooling as a youth or as
an old man. It is this schooling that will allow
him one day to awaken as the legitimate suc-
cessor and heir of a departed master; the departed master, in turn, will continue to remain
near the earth and, uniting with his succes-
sor's spirit, transmit to him his own perfected
mastery.

Only at this point does the one born to be a
master truly *become* a master, and only then
will he become conscious of his priesthood
"in the order of Melchizedek."*

During his years of maturation, the one born
to be a master must first pass through various phases of evolution—from occult to high
spiritual development—just as a child in its
mother's womb passes through all the stages
of evolution of the lower living beings that

---

* The Order of Melchizedek is referred to in Hebrews 7:13-17.
Jesus is considered to be a priest in the order of Melchizedek
because he is both priest and king in one, and his priesthood is
not based on being a descendant of Aaron, which is the lineage
required under Mosaic law.

precede that of the human, until it finally takes the form of a human being.

Thus, the still unperfected master reaches a point of decision, at which time he is free to choose between becoming a fakir or becoming a spiritual master.

He has discovered powers within himself that would have made it easy for him to perform hitherto unheard-of feats—feats that would seem like miracles to others—and the temptation to remain at the level of fakir is great. Insofar as he possesses the inner strength to withstand this temptation he proves himself to be one of those very rare individuals who are truly *chosen*. In doing so he places an inviolable seal on the occult fakir powers of his nature that will bind them for all time, unless the most holy Oldest One of the brothers on earth, who abides within the realm of pure radiant Spirit, gives him permission, sanctioned by the Spirit, to remove this seal. This event, however, may occur only once during millennia, and then only in the service of a mission that cannot be accomplished in any other way.

However, a true master would never in all Eternity be given permission to launch a "movement" like the one started by the woman who founded the Theosophical Society under the auspices of her supposed "masters." Never would permission be given so that absurd, spiritistic feats involving teacups and letters could be performed—antics that are secretly laughed at by any fakir or sorcerer-lama. I hope the reader will appreciate my irony.

It is almost inconceivable that serious people would be totally swayed by such reported phenomena—and could seriously believe that a *purely spiritual* community, of high ethical standing and also wholly rooted in the spiritual life of the cosmos, would indulge in this sort of rubbish in order to demonstrate its "sovereignty over natural laws" in such a trivial manner.

⚬

THE POWERS that a Mediator of Eternal Light possesses on earth—one who is born to be a master and has been perfected in a mortal human; a true master of the spiritual "White Lodge," if we are to stay with this commonly used though purely arbitrary term as a help to understanding—would hardly be suited to bringing about external phenomena so that he might enter into competition with the first reasonably skilled fakir who comes along.

In his external life on earth every real spiritual master is subject to the same laws of nature as the rest of humankind. He has long ago voluntarily renounced the use of powers through which, as a declared or secret fakir, he could have gained the reputation of a miracle worker.

In exchange for this renunciation, however, he has acquired a power which, like the queen bee in a hive, unites innumerable other forces and subordinates them under it so that they serve only the master's will. It is a power that would lead to the ruin of all others who might try to use it.

The effects of this sublime power and the forces subordinate to it extend into the physical world of manifestation, but their origin cannot be discerned in that world. Only those who were born to be Mediators of Eternal Light and who also have achieved mastery through many years of schooling may consciously access the sphere from which this sublime power originates, in order to set these forces in motion.

The spirit of each human being penetrates this sublime sphere, albeit not consciously, and thus—although they cannot initiate activity from here—the possibility arises that every human being can be *influenced* from here.

❧

MOST INDIVIDUALS REMAIN unaffected by inspiration from this sphere because their higher spiritual faculties are locked in a kind of rigor mortis. In every age, however, there also are many whose higher spiritual faculties are already awakened, although this activity may not yet register within the person's brain-based consciousness.

These more mature souls who, through work on themselves guided by good instincts, achieve an involuntary, spontaneous awakening of their higher spiritual faculties, form the true community of those who experience the spiritual influence of the Mediators of Eternal Light—although they are not aware of this in their mortal consciousness.

This influence can be *consciously* felt only when the higher spiritual faculties of such a person have sufficiently developed and when the will, now roused from its slumber, is ready to devotedly follow through on all inspirations that are received from higher spiritual spheres. Such persons will be shielded from the dangers that threaten unprepared souls when the higher spiritual faculties begin to awaken.

Nature protects vulnerable, mortal beings by insuring that none are born into this world with fully awakened higher spiritual senses. Long years of persevering work on oneself are required for this awakening to occur. Those who pursue this path will not truly awaken until they have withstood the trials that will vouchsafe that they have developed sufficient moral integrity to use their spiritual senses for good.

Were it not for these protections, the higher spiritual faculties of human beings that can give rise to their greatest bliss might plunge them into desperation and despair. They might suffer the pain of spiritual annihilation without even realizing what they have brought upon themselves.

On the other hand, one should not think that those who have not yet awakened but who, nevertheless, already receive the spiritual influence of the masters are not in any way conscious of that help.

To be sure, such influence is *felt*—although most are not aware of its origin. They look to superstitious or religious beliefs or dry, logical causes in an effort to explain it when, in fact, the help they are receiving from lofty, spiritual heights is coming from the Elder Brethren.

This influence does not, as one might think, consist of knowledge that flows from the font of wisdom that a spiritual master possesses—although this kind of influence is not absolutely excluded in individuals who have achieved a high level of inner development. Rather, in most cases this influence consists of a transmission of helping energies emanating from the spiritual realm. These helping energies enable those who receive them to become aware, through their higher spiritual faculties, of their *own* higher impulses.

It has been said that the Mediators of Eternal Light are able to spiritually reach all peoples and every single individual. But even though entire peoples have been under their influence for long stretches at a time, this contact

happened only because there were many individuals among the totality who were able
to enter into the spiritual sphere of influence
of the Masters of Light. This *purely spiritual*
community does not entertain any sort of
preference or prejudice regarding particular
peoples, nations, or races; it is concerned
only with individuals. Race, nationality or af-
filiation with a particular group is absolutely
irrelevant on the sublime spiritual level where
those who mediate eternal Light work—the
masters do not even recognize such earthly
distinctions. Here is where a true *universal
fellowship* of all those able to enter the sacred
realm truly reigns. Destructive forces cannot
come near to it or be assimilated within it, due
to their aversion to the Light that emanates
from this sacred sphere.

❦

IN THESE LOFTY SPIRITUAL SPHERES "freedom" exists only insofar it can be achieved
within the strictures of cosmic law. Here
"equality" has never existed nor will it ever
exist because in these regions the law of *hierarchy* prevails, wherein all individuals must
take their given places according to the in-
exorable demands of cosmic necessity. The

Gothic cathedral is the most perfect reflection of this hierarchical, cosmic order: the stones from which the outer walls are built number in the thousands, the stones that can be used for the buttresses and for the pinnacles of the towers are far fewer in number and, finally, only a single stone forms the finial.

As varied as the shape and beauty of these stones may be, they are all equally *needed* to achieve the harmonious balance of the whole—and only in this respect can one speak of "equality." Each stone has a rank within the whole and is subordinate to that order, from the finial at the top and the widely visible pinnacles of the towers down to the most hidden stones of the foundation, which have no other task but to support the entire edifice.

It is no different in the realm of Spirit, whose timeless harmony is secured by the unerring workings of the law of hierarchy.

Staying with the image of the Gothic cathedral, one might describe the hidden task of the Mediators of Eternal Light as being "master builders" of the Temple who send spiritual help that assists individual "stones" engaged in the work of "stonemasonry" to form themselves. It would be useless for a spiritually alive "stone," which may be indispensable as one of the many stones in a bearing wall supporting the vault of the cathedral, to lament the fact that it is not a buttress or a pinnacle stone.

The knowledge that an authentic master of the art of *cosmic* architecture possesses—one who is in possession of its timeless blueprints—is an absolutely certain knowledge of the soul's eternal nature. It is not dependent on some mental process of planning or calculation nor is it knowledge in the sense of any earthly discipline.

An example may illustrate this point: Every child or ordinary person with healthy eyes knows that they are able to see when their eyelids are opened. From a scientist's point of view, however, the activity that we refer to as "seeing" is extremely complex and much study is needed to completely understand its workings.

The masters regard "seeing" in the same way as does the child or the ordinary person.

They want nothing more than to be able to see and it is enough for them to know that they see.

In the realm of Spirit, a scientific analysis of seeing would be useless and, beyond that, even harmful in the extreme. This is because, in the spiritual realm, one cannot separate an activity from the analysis of that activity—as one can do on earth—and analysis would nullify the activity and render it impossible.

In the transcendent realm of radiant Spirit absolute certainty can be found only in a state of complete naïveté. Much of what science deems important to investigate—so much so that some pious scientists even presume to believe that they will find conclusive answers when they reach the life beyond—is of no importance whatsoever in the spiritual realm. There such matters are considered not worth knowing and even reprehensible.

The Mediators of Eternal Light consider the quest to increase knowledge through analytical thinking to be nothing other than the *calamity* that drove human beings out of "paradise." They view it as an expression of sheer folly, akin to someone who, in order to discover the hidden mechanism of a clock, immerses it in a vat of strong acid, hoping to gain insights once it has dissolved into atoms.

In the transcendent spheres, the search for knowledge through analytical thinking leads in the precisely *opposite* direction from the result that is desired. Cosmic law causes forms to spring into being from points of energy amid the unformed sea of chaos and the meaning of these forms can only be truly understood in their most sublime, spiritual manifestation. In these spheres every higher form illuminates its lower manifestation, but the attempt to draw conclusions about the higher from its lower embodiment—although it may seem to render satisfactory results within certain limits—will lead to false conclusions.

This is the reason why no authentic spiritual master would ever devote more attention to the everyday events of his generation—which, given his concept of time, only represents a tiny *atom* of time—than is absolutely necessary for his personal life on earth.

❦

For an authentic spiritual master, remnants of atavistic, occult abilities such as clairvoyance and the like are precluded, right from birth, by virtue of his psychophysical nature.

There is no surer sign of a false master, even if he honestly believes himself to be a true one, than the fact that he is known as being a clairvoyant.

At best, clairvoyants see hidden things which belong to the realm of the invisible, *physical* world. They may believe they are perceiving spiritual phenomena, but this is a delusion. In fact, they are merely seeing the reflections of mental constructs created by human beings here on earth. These images and ideas saturate the invisible, *physical* aura of this planet.

There never has been an authentic spiritual master who was omniscient. Any tales of omniscience spread by superstitious enthusiasts or unscrupulous charlatans belong to the realm of fables.

If a true spiritual master here on earth displays unusual abilities with respect to matters of this earthly life then this is merely due to an inborn talent he possesses in his physical body. He never could avail himself of help from the occult without breaking the binding law he freely pledged himself to obey. It is through his adherence to this pledge that he stands or falls in his task.

❧

EVEN A SPIRITUAL MASTER may still fall. Only he, in his dimension as a mortal being, can commit the one "sin" for which there is no "absolution": to sin against the "Holy Spirit." Such a sin would consist of a defiant and arrogant ignoring of that which seeks to reveal itself through him. He would then disappear from the spiritual world without a trace—like a star, once extinguished, vanishes from the cosmos. His name would be deleted from "The Book of the Lamb"—the book with seven seals.*

To be sure, the *timeless essence* of such a criminal within the Spirit's realm can never be annihilated, even as a result of the spiritual suicide he has committed in his physical

---

* *The Book of the Lamb,* also known as *The Lamb's Book of Life,* is referred to in Revelations, chapters 5-8. Only those who have attained eternal life are inscribed in the book. The Lamb refers to Jesus, who is the only one worthy to open the seals of the book, and this opening marks the Second Coming. Bô Yin Râ is using these terms metaphorically.

dimension. However, his consciousness of himself as a distinct, individuated being will gradually decompose over millennia and dissolve into the universal, planetary consciousness. As his self-knowledge fades, its last flicker will confirm to him that he has condemned himself to descend into the darkness of a harrowing night.

He is "Lucifer," the fallen bearer of Light who once stood before the very throne of God. As long as human beings inhabit the earth, there also is a "hell"—such a concept is not merely an invention of priests eager to control the masses. Nor is it a fantasy to say that this planet is surrounded by a host of "devils"— the fallen sons of God, who will not find peace until the depths of Chaos shall devour the last spark of their consciousness.

And "...the devil, as a roaring lion, walketh about the earth seeking whom he may devour." (1 Peter 5:8 KJV)

These fallen spirits procure their accomplices among living mortals on this earth by teaching their new-found disciples the very fakir arts which they themselves had once abjured.

They keep their disciples under the delusion that they did not "fall" but instead have risen above their former brothers, and convince them that their former brothers' self-imposed obedience to eternal laws is nothing more than adherence to a pious fraud.

Everything considered devilish, evil, and base on earth they declare to be permissible to their pupils. To this day they maintain a distorted, satanic version of the spiritual community of Light—both versions existing in the heart of Asia—a cesspool of abominations whose poisonous miasmas pollute the more susceptible human groups, including numerous unaware victims in the Western world. Included here are secret societies, fraternities and secret cults spread throughout Asia and other parts of this earth who—as part of their religious beliefs—consider the human being as something that should not exist although, characteristically, they mainly seek the eradication of the white races.[*]

---

[*] Bô Yin Râ is here singling out a secret society that harbors hate against white people—but he is equally adamant about the destructiveness of hatred against *any* race. In his books, Bô Yin Râ makes it clear that anyone who harbors hate against a particular race cannot develop spiritually and, further, that

I am well aware that many readers will be even more reluctant to accept these ideas than to believe what I have said about the White Lodge.

Readers are likely to suspect that the beliefs of ancient religions have simply reappeared in a new guise—beliefs that they hold to be mere superstitions.

However, the reverse is true. The teachers of the ancient religions, the priests of the ancient cults, were for the most part "initiates" and, therefore, their accounts impart a knowledge of Reality, albeit veiled.

I am not presenting some kind of fiction nor am I recounting fairytales. I am merely relating facts which cannot be made to vanish from the face of this earth by denying their veracity.

The indisputable prerogative a true spiritual master has over other human beings is his absolute certainty, through *experience,* concerning matters in the realm of radiant Spirit and his power, on a high spiritual plane, to create

---

one's race on earth is irrelevant in the realm of the Spirit (for example, see pages 50–51 of this chapter, paragraph beginning with "It has been said that the Mediators of Eternal Light...")

conditions through which harm may be prevented—as far as possible—in lower spiritual spheres, all the way down to the invisible physical aura of this planet.

The battle against his fallen, former brothers, who would drag down with them everything within their reach, is one of his most important tasks.

However, this battle cannot be fought offensively but only defensively—by preventing attacks. Therefore, to the degree that human beings can be made aware of the danger, this task will be made easier.

❧

HUMAN BEINGS of the present day will never be able to take the invisible dangers surrounding them seriously as long as the concept of "spiritual master" remains unclear and problematic.

As long as people with common sense are expected to believe in "masters" who live on this earth yet at the same time, like demigods, are above all earthly matters; as long as people are expected to believe in "mahatmas" who can outdo any Indian fakir in the degree of triviality of their feats; as long as people are even asked to regard the brotherhood of Luminaries as a "great school of natural science"*—which is presumed to know infinitely more than those who practice the natural sciences in our colleges—then no serious, thinking person can be faulted for smiling with condescension upon hearing tales of such a brotherhood.

Nonetheless, much remains "mysterious in the light of day"** regarding a true spiritual master. It is not necessary to further cloak his existence in layers of veil.

In everyday life he is a mortal like any other and must never misuse his purely spiritual abilities in order to better his human lot.

---

* The Great School of Natural Science was founded in California in 1883 by John E. Richardson. It emphasizes self-mastery through living in harmony with the laws of natural science and universal intelligence.

** "Mysterious in the light of day, nature retains her veil, despite our clamours: that which she does not willingly display cannot be wrenched from her with levers, screws and hammers." This quote from Goethe's *Faust* (Part 1) would have been familiar to educated Europeans in Bô Yin Râ's day.

He is by no means a "genius," much less a "saint," as a result of his high level of spiritual development.

Only trained eyes would be able to recognize him as he goes about his everyday life.

In everyday life he is an ordinary human being and nothing more.

He is a master only on the spiritual plane. The ability to be simultaneously conscious in both the earthly and the spiritual realms—living as a mortal human being while also working in the world of Spirit—he owes to the spiritual mastery to which he was born and to his strengthened will. This steadfast will, once readied for the task, enabled him to ascend through all the spirals of spiritual schooling, despite outer and inner obstacles and dangers, until his perfection as a master was attained.

What remains mysterious in earthly life, even to the masters themselves, is the ongoing spiritual connection between individual masters—even if located at opposite ends of the earth—and the connection of all masters with their hidden terrestrial center in the heart of Asia. To be sure, no real master would ever lift the veil of mystery here even if it were possible for him to do so. The catch-all term "telepathy" and all the nice explanations found in books on the occult can never explain this process to persons unable to participate in it themselves. For those who can, the practice alone is sufficient and they will never feel tempted to try to find a "scientific" explanation for it, simply to satisfy their own curiosity.

For all others, it should suffice to know that a member of the White Lodge—a true Mediator of Eternal Light—will never teach anything relating to purely spiritual matters, either through the spoken word or in writing, without the complete agreement of his brothers and their spiritual head who dwells in eternal, primordial Light.

A spiritual master possesses absolute certainty only with regard to spiritual matters. In all other matters the extent to which he can be taken seriously depends solely on the experience, knowledge and abilities he has acquired in the ordinary way in everyday life.

May these explanations serve to eliminate a blind spot in the spiritual "eyes" of the human beings of my time. This obscured vision is the reason their world view remains fragmented and incomplete, regardless of how logical and balanced it may otherwise appear.

Those who seek the Light may rest assured that their path is protected by the Masters of the Radiant Day—the master builders of humanity's eternal Temple—who have been entrusted with the "cornerstone" which in itself embodies the perfect proportions inherent in the world of Spirit.

❧

CHAPTER THREE

THEOSOPHY AND PSEUDO-THEOSOPHY

HOW THE WORD THEOSOPHY HAS COME TO BE DEVALUED

I F IT WERE POSSIBLE FOR THE PEOPLE OF the Western world to suddenly shake off the many narcotic stupors that rob them of any lasting clarity, they would recognize the dreadful darkness that surrounds them as regards spiritual knowledge—and they would shudder with horror.

"Christendom" supposedly reigns on this corner of the earth and its followers base their beliefs on the writings of the authors of the Gospels, who are referred to as the "Four Evangelists"—bringers of "glad tidings" and light for the illumination of the "heathens."

Yet, the Gospels tell us that their sublime Master said the following words to his disciples: "Unto you it is given to know the mysteries of the Kingdom of God: but to others in parables; that seeing they might not see, and hearing they might not understand." (Luke 8:10 KJV)

These would be hard and terrible words if all human beings—as many would like to believe—were indeed "equal before God," from which it would follow that these "others" should have exactly the same right to fathom "the mysteries of the Kingdom of God."

But the sacred texts upon which Christian doctrine is based know nothing of this "equality before God." They differentiate quite firmly and clearly between "the children of this world" and "the children of the light."

In these texts the Master warns: "Give not that which is holy unto the dogs, neither cast ye your pearls before swine…" (Matthew 7:6 KJV) These exhortations clearly show that he was not of the opinion that all human beings are "equal before God."

In the accounts of his life and death that have been handed down to us he remains *silent* to Pilate's question as to who he is; but to those who recognized "…for flesh and blood hath not revealed it unto thee, but my Father which is in heaven" (Matthew 16:17 KJV) he speaks from the full majesty of his being and confirms who he truly is:

"Ye call me Master and Lord: and ye say well; for so I am." (John 13:13 KJV)

But where in the four writings referred to as the Gospels can one find the words this Master would have spoken *only* to these trusted ones—those in whom he had chosen to confide?

Words can indeed be found that *hint* at teachings known to the disciples, but in vain will one search for the teachings themselves.

The Church of Rome is not in the wrong when it bases its understanding of the teachings of the Master of Nazareth not only on the written word but also on oral tradition. However, has not this tradition long been buried and distorted—even if perhaps here and there some last traces of its existence reach us today?

It is said that the Master of Nazareth—the Master of the Gospels—did not leave behind anything in writing.

Everyone is free to believe me or not when I say that on this small planet there live human beings who know with *absolute certainty* that the Master of Nazareth left behind written records of his secret teachings. The last of these writings were still extant until the time of the persecution of Christians and were destroyed in Rome by later disciples who had been entrusted with their care, so as to prevent them from falling into the hands of "heathens." The Gospel of St. John contains excerpts from these texts—those portions of the Master's writings that speak in veiled language and could be woven into the text as discourse.

Those who know this, also know that followers of the Master's teachings made copies of the teachings written in the Master's own hand and then disseminated them, and that excerpts from these copies can be found in other texts besides the Gospel of St. John.

❧

To be sure, this is not the full extent of the knowledge these few possess regarding the Master of the Gospels. However, just as was the case with the first of his disciples, they are bound by a law which obliges them to guard as secret that which cannot be revealed to all.

To the "others" they also speak using only parables and veiled symbols.

They are guardians of a sacred treasure—renewed with every generation—and preserved on this planet through them. They truly are the "Knights of the Holy Grail" referred to in legend. They perform a sacred task in service of the Spirit which very few individuals in every generation are qualified to carry out—because only very few are born to it.

One must be born to it just as one human being was born to be Mozart and another Beethoven while others can never be their equals—not with all the determination in the world.

The individuals I have referred to here—among whom persons of European blood have rarely appeared, even in the course of millennia—are at all times the only ones possessing, to either a greater or lesser degree, that secret knowledge which the Master of the Gospels possessed—and he possessed it only because he was one of them. But he also knew that there was another to whom he owed everything—as did his spiritual brothers—and who he honored and revered as being greater still than him.

He was empowered to prepare a "mansion in his father's house"* for each of his disciples and, so he has done. Even today he *lives* in his spiritual form among those who are his Father's sons. These few, born into the realm of eternal Spirit, remain in full possession of their powers even after their physical death and are not, like the others, subject to the laws of this planet.

They are the only true spiritual masters on this earth: the Mediators of Eternal Light, the living bearers of the eternal spirit of the Christos; the transformers of timeless, divine wisdom into that which may be humanly comprehended.

Those who find the above assertions to be unbelievable, or who feel their pious religious faith to be endangered, are free to doubt what they read; but they will not be able to alter in the slightest the reality upon which all that I have written here is based.

---

* "In my Father's house are many mansions: if it were not so, I would have told you. I go to prepare a place for you." (John 14:2 KJV) More modern translations use words like "room" or "dwelling place" instead of mansion, in order to better convey the meaning of the original Greek word.

There are thousands among the various Christian congregations who have developed their inner life and raised up their soul, so that they have been able to transcend the dogmas so zealously guarded by their churches. They are not paying homage to delusion when they truly feel the presence of their Master.

᪣

ONE SHOULD NOT ASSUME that the Mediators of Eternal Light, among whom the Master of Nazareth lives in his spiritual form even today on this earth, are the same as the "masters" certain so-called theosophical writings speak about. Nor should they be equated with the "Great School of Natural Science,"* created in the United States, which bears the stamp of falsity despite all the moral posing and high sounding explanations of its—now unmasked—inventor.

"For there shall arise false Christs and false prophets, and shall show great signs and wonders; insomuch that, if it were possible, they

---

* The Great School of Natural Science was founded in 1883 in California by John E. Richardson. Richardson was charged with financial mismanagement in 1916. However, he then reorganized the school and it survives to this day.

shall deceive the very elect." (Matthew 24:24 KJV)

But "...the children of this world are in their generation wiser than the children of light." (Luke 16:8 KJV)

The "Sons of the Light," the true emissaries of "Theo-Sophia" on this earth, are indeed possessed with knowledge, but it is of an entirely different kind than the knowledge one acquires from the study of science.

Despite the understandable skepticism that reasonable people may feel, I am obliged to assert the truth that a very few on this earth do, indeed, possess such hidden knowledge.

It is a kind of knowing that comes from gaining inner certitude through *experience* and cannot be attained by one who is not *born* with the capacity to achieve it. It is not knowledge "of" or "about" something but, rather, a knowing that takes place through a continuous, conscious, active process of *becoming one* with the object of the knowledge itself.

The Indian sage Patânjali describes it in this way: Just as water takes on the shape of the receptacle it fills, the spirit of the yogi takes on the shape of the object he wishes to comprehend. Needless to say, Patânjali is not referring to the kind of "yogi" found on street corners and at the entrances of temples.

The inner experience of those able to attain such knowledge may best be described as *knowing through transformation of the self.*

ॐ

APART FROM THIS spiritual knowledge there also is a "teaching" that cannot be transmitted in spoken words, nor could it ever be put into writing, because this teaching too can only be apprehended through inner experience. Since the dawn of time, this teaching has been passed down by awakened Masters, through a process of spiritual transmission, to those mortals who have become conscious of their transcendent humanity—their eternal soul.

Only those who have a natural affinity are able to receive this sacred, wordless teaching and there are more human beings able to *come* to know through this kind of "teaching" than there are those *born* to know through transformation of the self.

There is an innermost, hidden realm of spirit and there are sublime, powerful beings who reside in the spiritual sphere of this planet to whom all who live on this earth owe that which is finest and best in their being.

There is an eternal life *from* which the human spirit enters into this world of matter and an eternal life *to* which it returns after physical death.

There are spiritual "wonders" that eclipse any exotic fairytale and yet they are realities.

But everything that may be said about these things in words and whatever has flowed down from the eternal realm through the sublime hierarchy of spiritual beings dwelling in eternal Light, all the way to the Mediators of Eternal Light on earth and into the channel of human language, is unspeakably little compared to what those who know through transformation of the self owe to their *experience*. They truly are entitled to say, as did the Master of the Gospels: "All things that the Father hath are mine" and "I and the Father are one." (John 16:15; John 10:30 KJV)

The community of those few who know through transformation of the self is the representation of the spirit of the eternal Christos on this earth and the Master of the Gospels is one of the highest sons of this spiritual community—the Mediators of Eternal Light who alone *know* the "Father" and thus can *do* as the "Father" teaches them.*

Yet the pious people of his time called the Master of Nazareth "a glutton and a drunkard" because they could not understand how a "godly" person can live with "sinners" and how it is that he does not disdain the gifts of this earth.**

They could not see that in him the "kingdom of the heavens," had come nigh, in the midst of earthly life. Nor could they exclaim, as Cephas-Peter did: "Lord, to whom shall we go? thou hast the words of eternal life." (John 6:68 KJV)

---

* "Then answered Jesus and said unto them, Verily, verily, I say unto you, the Son can do nothing of himself, but what he seeth the Father do: for what things soever he doeth, these also doeth the Son likewise." (John 5:19 KJV)

** "The Son of man came eating and drinking, and they say, Behold a man gluttonous and a winebibber, a friend of publicans and sinners. But wisdom is justified of her children." (Matthew 11:19 KJV)

❧

Bᴜᴛ ᴛʜᴇ "Sᴏɴ ᴏꜰ Gᴏᴅ" of the Gospels never considered himself to be the *sole* bearer of divine sonship here on earth.

Those who came after him misunderstood his words, believing that he and he alone bore this sacred role, and reinterpreted his teachings in accordance with their own understanding.

Countless errors have resulted from the failure to comprehend the mystery of the Christos and many an incorrect teaching could have been avoided if one had understood the *true* meaning of the words: "I am the door: by me if any man enter in, he shall be saved and shall go in and out, and find pasture." (John 10:9 KJV)

Thus, the stone which was set as the cornerstone was rejected by the builders.* And seekers set out on false paths, for the path which is truth and life seems to them impassible.

❧

---

* "This is the stone which was set at nought of you builders, which is become the head of the corner." (Acts 4:11 KJV)

The section that follows contains material that may be confusing or even offensive to some. Readers should keep in mind that Bô Yin Râ's purpose—implied at the start of the following section and made specific later—is to discredit Helena Blavatsky and the spread of the Theosophical movement. In our day it is hard to imagine the extent to which Madame Blavatsky's ideas held sway; they were regarded as the ultimate revelations of truth and were spreading rapidly throughout the world. Bô Yin Râ considered Blavatsky's influence to be pernicious and a menace to truth; he was convinced that her writings were filled with misinformation and, most importantly, that she had the potential to unleash destructive, occult powers that could endanger the entire world, without she herself realizing the consequences. —The Editors

IN OUR DAY, most people consider it only just that men and women be treated as equals. The admonition that a woman should "keep silent in the churches" and not teach in the congregation* is considered to be an outdated concept,

---

* "Let your women keep silence in the churches: for it is not permitted unto them to speak; but they are commanded to be under obedience as also saith the law." (1 Corinthians 14:34 KJV)

unworthy of a woman's nature, to be laughed at and regarded with scorn. However, the one who uttered these words was a true spiritual pupil of his Master and, therefore, knew that to be a master—a Mediator of Eternal Light— or his adopted pupil one must possess a male body. Only a Luminary or his adopted son can gather direct knowledge either through spiritual transmission or through transformation of the self.*

The burden of sacred knowledge that binds those who have attained it through spiritual transmission or through transformation of the self obliges them to accept the truth of St. Paul's words, which are still valid today and will be for millennia to come. This despite their deep honoring of women based on reverence for the Feminine.

---

* The fact that women cannot gather knowledge in these exceptional ways is based, according to Bô Yin Râ, on immutable physical and spiritual laws. However, both women and men are equally able to pursue the inner path in the manner that is open to everyone. For more on this see chapters 2 and 3 in *The Book on Human Nature*.

It is not without reason that in India the Lingam and in Ancient Greece the Phallus were considered to be the most sacred of all spiritual symbols. Even those individuals who have attained only an exoteric knowledge of the ancient Asiatic cults have nevertheless recognized that it is only possible to possess certain esoteric, high spiritual powers if one possesses in the flesh what these symbols represent.

Hermaphrodites have always been excluded from the "mysteries"—even from the most introductory ones. Only men could become initiates; women were only ever admitted to the preliminary stages of instruction—even though one had at all times gladly given to women whatever they could carry. Those mystery cults which had begun to admit women were in fact degenerate: the ability to realize the true mystery within had been desecrated by them and had therefore already long ago become inaccessible to them.

The highest, most sublime mysteries, in whatever form they may have appeared in human history, are always in their essence sacred spiritual-sexual mysteries. Kundalini—in the form of the male procreative power transformed into spirit—is venerated as holy among natives of India and regarded as the highest of all yogic powers. Needless to say, those knowledgeable about such transformation are not to be found among the yogis encountered by tourists.

If spiritual powers are to manifest on the physical plane, one must have physical organs that correspond to those powers.

The concept of a female "spiritual master" is a contradiction in terms because a woman can never possess the physical prerequisites that would allow her to attain a master's ability to know. Such ability requires intact male sexual organs.

A woman may be born a somnambulist or a seer but never could she become an initiate.

A woman, without exception, reaches her highest spiritual state only after her life on earth by becoming one with a male pole, thus forming a divinely transfigured human spirit. Through the mystery of this sacred union he carries her within himself—as if in a tabernacle—enveloped in love, throughout the infinity of the spiritual spheres.[*]

One simply need consider the various types of men portrayed in the Gospels, beginning with the Master and then down to the most distant of his disciples, and their powerful words—after they had reached maturity—with the women depicted alongside them. Only thus can one understand the way in which a woman can find her place if the mystery of the Christos is to touch her existence.

❧

THE POLARITY that each individual carries is timeless in nature beginning from its source in the innermost of Light eternal.

Never has a woman been a man in a former incarnation and never could she become a man

---

[*] In others of his writings, Bô Yin Râ makes it clear that the opposite is also true: a man also reaches his highest spiritual state only after his life on earth by becoming one with a female pole. For men, however, there is an exception: Luminaries, who are always in male bodies while living here on earth, are already united with a spark of the divine Feminine. For more on this see *The Book on Human Nature* and *The Book on Marriage*.

in a future incarnation, as popular pseudo-wisdom would have one believe.[*]

That which is male here on earth has always been of male polarity throughout Eternity, issuing from the male aspect of the Godhead, and that which is female here on earth has always been of female polarity, issuing from the feminine aspect of the Godhead—and the Godhead, itself, is eternally male *and* female.

The assumption that the polarity of the sexes is based solely on their physical nature, and can therefore change in a future incarnation, is absurd. It reveals an ignorance of the primary laws of the Spirit through which the polarity of gender—including that of the entire non-human physical world—is eternally determined.

That some women "would rather be men" has its basis in their feminine spiritual nature.

---

[*] Bô Yin Râ is countering the theosophist belief that a soul that is incarnated in a male body in one life can be reincarnated in a female body in another life. As in the previous section, his underlying purpose is to discredit Madame Blavatsky's claim to authority. Since Luminaries are incarnated in male bodies, logic would dictate that Blavatsky cannot be one of them.

Had they actually ever *been* men in a prior life, such a wish would be foreign to them.*

Moreover, that which is reincarnated, in all but a few exceptional cases, are the *soul forces*; that is, soul forces that have not been fulfilled by the human being who generated them will pass on to another human being, reappearing again and again in new human beings until their energy has been exhausted.

These soul forces can, of course, be transferred from men to women and from women to men—when the impulse is released by its present carrier, upon that person's death—without, however, changing the gender of their carriers.

Every human being is a unique emanation of the eternal Spirit, imbued with a will towards individuation, and "charged" with male or female polarity, even though there are feminine

---

* The meaning of these two sentences is opaque. Bô Yin Râ seems to be alluding to the fact that Theosophists believe this kind of wish proves that such a woman has spent many of her previous lifetimes in a succession of male bodies. Bô Yin Râ's own very different explanation is set out in the two paragraphs that follow. Read in the context of the entirety of his writing, one could also surmise that he would have said the same of men.

elements alive in the male and male elements alive in the female. Human beings who have completed their paths on earth shall never, under normal circumstances, return again as mortals at a later time.

Those cases in which reincarnation actually occurs in the crude sense described in popular lore are certain abnormal situations: suicide, infant death, or the case of a person who has regressed to an altogether animalistic level. These exceptional cases are hardly important to consider because, here too, there can never be a change of the polarity of gender which, once given, is fixed for all Eternity.

When people today use the term "theosophy" they usually mean something quite different from what I refer to and the pious supporters of today's "secret doctrines" will see in my words an attack on their most cherished dogma.

But, then, who was it that gave the world these "secret doctrines" in such abundance?

Do not all these teachings with their supposed "unveiling" of secret wisdom, which have captivated countless souls for almost half a century, proceed from one particular woman?

In a certain sense she was indeed a brilliant woman who, as a result of her somnambulistic predisposition, was able to grasp fragments of true wisdom. However, being a woman, she could not cope with the energies needed for this purpose and was compelled to let her soul be used by men who wielded certain powers— and these men severely misused their power over her. Eventually, those with spiritual authority found it necessary to lead her into error because she was coming too close to knowing secrets that would have unleashed destructive forces: She would have become a danger to the entire world without realizing the far-reaching consequences of what she was doing.

It was this woman whose ambition moved her to attempt to give what only those can give who know through *transformation of the self*. And those who know through transformation of the self would never have presented what they know in a form that *she* would have chosen.

❧

Nowadays people say: She was only an instrument in the hands of her "masters," whom she served with deep devotion.

Regrettably, this is only too true and for this reason her gift—which she offered with a mixture of presumption and blind faith—became a Trojan horse.

Her writings weave together fragments of timeless wisdom with the superstitions of all ages and regions.

One may find there hints of highest wisdom but enveloped by a fog of pseudo-knowledge, bred in the darkest tombs of human aberrance—passed on to her by those who considered it sacred but, in fact, was the end result of sacrificing all that is truly most sacred in the human spirit.

Her writings contain traces from ancient, true spiritual paths obscured by explanations that are parodies of truth, given to her in order to fool her.

The disparate nature of her output corresponds to the disparate sources of her inspirations.

❧

THIS UNFORTUNATE WOMAN seems to have been a sort of living "radio receiver" forced to pick up everything that reached her, from all over the world and beyond, because of her abnormal predisposition to somnambulism and to serving as a medium.

However, she was without the means to verify her sources and control them.

She trustingly believed in the "towering wisdom" transmitted to her, among other things, from a source which even today takes peculiar pleasure in parodying the *The Western Wisdom Teachings*[*] and deploys all its occult wiles to this end, in spiritist sessions or wherever it can get hold of a European who is predisposed by nature to be a medium. Of course, those who are not familiar with this extrasensory realm from their own experience will consider all these spiritistic manifestations to be quite wondrous, without realizing that they themselves may have fallen victim to such questionable sources.

With complete passivity, this woman succumbed to the influence of another secret sect

---

[*] *The Western Wisdom Teachings*, also known as *The Rosicrucian Cosmo-Conception*, is the central text of the Rosicrucian Fellowship, a Rosicrucian order founded in 1909 by Max Heindel and influenced by the philosophy of the Theosophical Society. Rosicrucians blend Christian doctrine with the belief that their members possess secret knowledge handed down to them from ancient times.

which is widespread in Asia but has its deepest roots in certain regions of Tibet. This sect considers it their *religious duty* to mobilize all their ample occult means in order to cause harm to Europeans and, if possible, to annihilate them.

At the same time she was also influenced by well-intentioned, yet misguided, enthusiasts who sought to rescue her from this danger but, instead of the gold of true insight, had only fool's gold to offer. Moreover, their help was troubling in that they fostered in this object of their influence the belief that certain other manifestations of a *physical* nature that had greatly impressed her emanated from them—and thus used these manifestations to lead her in a direction that suited their own purposes.

Disarmed by these appeals to her vanity, this tormented woman was unable to think critically, and was inclined to consider *all* these manifestations as coming from the highest and most sublime source. And although she had learned of the existence of this source while in a somnambulistic state, she had never come into *direct* contact with it.

A veritable witches sabbath of occult influences descended upon the excitable soul of this pitiable woman. Had Richard Hodgson[*] known the full extent of what was happening to this woman he would have been able to add some unique reports to the "Proceedings of the Society of Psychical Research," unmatched in interest by anything else to be found in the entire world. However, he was only able to uncover her more obvious attempts at deception. I encourage the reader to look at his reports.

As I have already stated, those who have authority in these matters and could see the danger she posed were obligated to cause all communication to this woman to be confused because it touched on certain things that needed to remain secret. This secrecy was of utmost importance for without it horrendous occult forces of explosion and dissolution might be added to the already terrible wealth

---

[*] Richard Hodgson was an Australian-born psychical researcher who had a role in exposing several fraudulent mediums. In 1884 he was sent by the Society for Psychical Research to investigate Madame Blavatsky, and concluded that her claims of psychic powers were fraudulent.

of destructive inventions that Western "culture" possesses.

Just as fire and electricity may act as beneficent servants of humanity but are also capable of destroying everything we hold dear, such forces can be a blessing when handled by responsible individuals who are called to do this work, but can turn into forces of destruction in the hands of all others, even if this is not their intention.

Given these influences and counter-influences, it is easy to see that the writings of this strange woman and the reports about her life are overrun by a thicket of jungle-like overgrowth and choked by entangling vines—and that this result was inevitable.

✍

From this tropical jungle of fantastical flowers and orchids with numbing fragrance, wreaths have been fashioned. Since the earthly days of this unfortunate, somnambulist seer, her followers believed they must lay them as an offering on the altars of the temples of the "masters."

Virtually everything that has usurped the name "theosophy" since her time is based on the teachings of this seemingly adventurous and mysterious woman.

Men who felt themselves drawn to this woman, her writings or accounts about her life, because of their own somnambulist predisposition, were subject to the same influences as she was. As a result, they "confirmed" through what they termed "scientific spiritual investigation" what their prophetess, glowing in the fires of the underworld, had proclaimed.

Women of a highly sensitive nature and filled with great fervor immersed themselves so completely in the conceptual world of their famous idol that they soon learned to "see" everything in the way that *Helena Petrovna Blavatsky* would have things be seen. Such was the force of her authority that any expression of doubt about her assertions seemed to them a blasphemy against spiritual truth.

☙

AND SO IN TIME the ground was prepared on which the most diverse of spiritual parasites could thrive and spread, and infect others unhindered. It was all too easy to find support for any sort of teachings, however abstruse, in passages from the writings of the "servant of the masters" or to present those teachings as the latest results of "scientific spiritual research."

The latter method was especially effective since the label "scientific spiritual research" inspired feelings of trust in Westerners who, accustomed to the precise scientific research methods of the natural sciences, could be taken in by the pronouncements of an especially skilled juggler of concepts, without a second thought. At best, these "findings" were merely the product of the "spiritual investigator's" self-hypnosis but, most unfortunately, their "research results" led to many *collective* hypnoses, aided by various secondary means.

Anyone familiar with the history of the Anglo-Indian "theosophical" movement and its impact will easily find examples of what I am referring to.

The fact that this movement could spread throughout India does not reflect favorably on the discernment of modern, half-Europeanized Indians. To be sure, the discernment of many Europeans is not much better—we see them running in droves after all sorts of self-proclaimed visionaries or money-seeking, world traveling Asian imposters, especially if these supposed "seers," "masters," "yogis" or whatever else they may call themselves wear an exotic caftan and are, preferably, also dark-skinned.

Whoever is able to read the writings of this movement's founder with something other than pious awe and reverence—those who dare to analyze these writings *critically* and who examine the accounts about the life of their author with the same discerning attitude—will soon be in a position to verify everything that I have said about the sources of her inspiration. They will also soon discover that the attempt to portray this unfortunate woman as a victim of European occultists—which caused something of a stir at the time—was based on a complete inability to penetrate the reality that underlay the situation: the fact that she herself was a medium.

❧

Reasonable, discriminating individuals will hardly require me to account for the sources of my knowledge in this matter.

One may, of course, doubt everything I have said so far, should one, after having verified what is easily verifiable, still dare to do so. The fact that I am speaking with absolute certainty—fully aware of my responsibility—will most likely not have escaped those who, for their own reasons, would have much preferred that these words had never been written at all.

I, too, would have much preferred not to write them. I would have rather kept my knowledge quietly to myself, if it had not been my obligation to write it down.

I am speaking with the approval of those whose existence Madame Blavatsky intuited while in a somnambulistic state—those beings with whom she believed herself to be in direct contact but never truly was—not even in some trance state and also not in her outer life.

Our knowledge is not based on observation of the external world but comes, rather, from a mode of perception where the truth is never veiled—unlike perception that is transmitted through the physical senses.

In the name of those who know through transformation of the self and whose silent, concealed spiritual community has outlasted many millennia, I hereby declare that *Helena Petrovna Blavatsky* erred when she believed herself to have ever come into direct occult or external contact with one of us. She had no idea who her inspirers really were—the inspirers of the teachings she referred to as "Theosophy." And the society she took over and called "Theosophical" originally bore a different name, and openly called itself "spiritualist."

The teachings promulgated by her are a hodgepodge of heterogeneous ideas drawn from all times and peoples, augmented by the additions of her publisher and those of her English and other Western friends. They have so little in common with true theosophy—as this word has been understood since its dissemination through Paul the Apostle and for centuries since—that using this word to describe her teachings is nothing less than a corruption of the term.

Genuine theosophy can easily clad itself in an assortment of religious robes but never can a cloak patched together from scraps of priestly garments, scavenged from all the world's religions, bestow upon its wearer "theo-sophia"— a knowledge of God.

Lao-Tzu, the great Indian and Tibetan religious teachers, the Apostle Paul and the author of the Gospel of St. John are among those who proclaimed *true* theosophy. Included here also are the authentic, wisdom-drunk Muslim Sufis of ancient Persia; the last Indian prophet, Ramakrishna; the mystical philosophers Tauler and Meister Eckhart and the still very little understood Jakob Boehme, whose soul was from birth destined to become open to the Spirit. But to declare the results of occult possession found in the *The Secret Doctrine* of Madame Blavatsky to be "theosophy"—that is the height of nonsense.

The real benefit that has come from this enterprising woman is that she provided the Western world with clues as to the existence of a source of wisdom located in the "innermost East." Like a would-be Moses leading her people to the promised land, she sensed its existence but never truly saw it. Never did the waters of its sacred wellspring moisten her impetuous tongue.

❧

IN MY WRITING I HAVE SHOWN, again and again, how one may truly come closer to this pure source of sacred waters which "flows from high mountains."*

Those who would find this source must search within and from there begin to climb the steep, ascending path that leads one to it.

They may, without a qualm, remain within the faith that they have known since childhood and translate what I offer in my writings into that faith's venerable concepts. They should keep in mind, however, that I write first and foremost for those individuals who are not satisfied with the prevailing forms of faith and yet still seek to find their living God within.

Those who believe they need more guidance and are also able to read between the lines—with a sober, clear-minded attitude and awareness of the time and place in which

---

* "And there shall be upon every high mountain, and upon every high hill, rivers and streams of waters in the day of the great slaughter, when the towers fall." (Isaiah 30:25 KJV)

things were written—need only explore the writings of the above-mentioned mystical philosophers. They may certainly add to this list the writings of Angelus Silesius and Thomas à Kempis.

They should select whatever speaks to their soul wherever they may find it. But they should avoid the error of believing that those things the soul knows—the *true theosophy* to be found among all peoples and in every age—is the sort of knowledge that can be gained through scholarship. It is also an error to think that the knowledge of the timeless soul needs support from any external source; that it can be furthered by the efforts of a worldly association or gained by the study of weighty tomes. One could spend a lifetime acquainting oneself with the testimonies written by those who had truly become alive in the Spirit—but a life spent in such a way would lead one far from the soul's path towards the Light. All those who have dedicated their lives to such investigations have departed from this earth with their souls destitute and lost in deepest anguish.

"…seek, and ye shall find; knock, and it shall be opened unto you." (Matthew 7:7 KJV)

But only steadfast perseverance when seeking and when knocking within leads to the goal to which the Master of the Gospels directed his chosen few when he said: "He that believeth on me, believeth not on me, but on him that sent me." (John 12:44 KJV)

"For I have not spoken of myself; but the Father which sent me, he hath given me a commandment, what I should say, and what I should speak. And I know that his commandment is life everlasting: whatsoever I speak therefore, even as the Father said unto me, so I speak."(John 12:49-50, KJV)

With these words he spoke for all those who *know* the "Father," whether they manifest in a mortal body in India, China, Tibet, or in modern Europe. The words of all who teach as the Father would have them teach lead to true "theo-sophia," which is identical to the everlasting, mystery-filled "Christendom" of the spiritual realm emanating from the eternal Christos dwelling in the primordial Light. The most sublime Temple of the eternal Christos on earth has existed in the "innermost East" long before the Master of Nazareth—as a member of this Temple—taught how to experience timeless love. This Temple will remain until the end of days on this earth and with it for time *eternal* will remain those who have been entrusted with this Temple's duties by the divine—those who have been ordained as "priests according to the order of Melchizedek": the "order" through which the Eternal places itself within the realm of time.

Only those few mortals whose timeless, spiritual being has received the needed form of consciousness from the Sophia—the timeless feminine pole of the radiant Spirit, which is the wisdom that is God's—have the ability, in accordance with this priestly order, to impart to their fellow human beings an understanding and knowledge of the Sophia.

CHAPTER FOUR

THE THREE LEVELS
OF BEING

Although we are surrounded by a world that reveals itself only through our physical senses—senses that are themselves a part of this external world—human experience is by no means limited to life within the physical realm.

The intellect may seek to penetrate the inner workings of the physical world, and science may probe its secrets, yet deeper layers remain closed to all such explorations.

In the innermost regions of this world mysterious forces, known to but a few, perpetually create and give rise to material forms. Time and again human beings are misled into believing that these forces can be mastered. But in truth these forces obey only their *own* innate laws and, sooner or later, must destroy any who are foolhardy enough to think they can interfere with what nature has set in place.

This occult realm of nature, of which I speak, has never brought gain to anyone who strayed into it.

Like a fly caught in a spider's web, anyone who dares to venture too far into this realm will be caught, cocooned and sucked dry.

And just as a large insect will shake the spider's web in which it has been caught, foolhardy inquirers shake the web woven by nature's occult forces—while their followers stare in amazement and say: "Look how this expert is able to master the forces of the occult!"

These admirers do not suspect that such deluded investigators merely disturb the threads that hold them captive—and which soon will bind and ruin them completely. Thus doomed, the victims seek also to lure others onto the path to destruction.

The breadth and depth of human existence cannot be fathomed by observing nature with one's physical senses or even by probing the occult forces at nature's core—even though it is true that humankind can manifest in the material world only through these occult forces and is itself an expression of these forces.

To be sure, human beings are themselves one expression of these occult forces of nature, but they are also, at the same time, something more.

∞

I CERTAINLY CAN UNDERSTAND why people say: "The supernatural does not exist; even the most incomprehensible occurrences are still within the bounds of nature." In this way they attempt to defend their belief in the unity of all living things.

But we deceive ourselves with such words. There truly is something entirely different in character from everything that we commonly consider to be within the realm of nature—no matter how broadly one defines that term.

There truly is something that does *not* lie within the domain of events we recognize as being governed by natural laws—something that obeys laws entirely different from what we consider to be part of nature.

If we regard something so completely different from nature as being part of nature then we confuse concepts that in reality are quite distinct, in spite of the overarching unity of all things that exist.

Such confusion is furthered by the inability of most humans to perceive the timeless, primal forces of Being—the occult forces—which are the only real constant underlying the ever-changing manifestations of nature.

Very few on this earth suspect what effects these forces are capable of bringing about, and that a great deal that is referred to as being "supernatural" is in fact the result of these forces.

Thus it is with good reason that even the most mysterious occurrences are often viewed as being rooted in nature. However, there also exist regions of Being far beyond even the most mysterious manifestations of the unseen physical realm. These regions will elude our understanding as long as we consider them to be part of the natural world, in which physical laws determine the unfolding of events.

❧

To DESCRIBE THESE HIGHER REGIONS I would use two words: "soul" and "spirit."

In recent times, many consider what is meant by the word "soul" to be loftier than what is meant by the word "spirit." However, I believe that the genesis of the word "soul" within the German language justifies my using this word to describe that flowing, luminous realm that lies *between* what is generally referred to as "physical nature" and that other realm: the realm of highest power and wisdom—the realm of Spirit.

The realm of the soul resembles a fluid sea of forces filled with mystery, permeated and illuminated by the realm of Spirit. These forces surpass everything that can be found within the region of the occult forces of physical nature and are completely independent of the laws that govern the natural world.

The human being is at home in the region of physical nature but also in this realm of soul. Here too, the human being is a part of the vast and immeasurable whole, for the soul that belongs to it is composed of countless forces from the ever-flowing sea of the soul.

In this region that lies between nature and Spirit human beings have the right to subjugate these soul forces to their will; here it is *imperative* that they learn to master these forces.

⁊

THE REALM OF THE SOUL lies between the forces of physical nature and those of the radiant realm of Spirit and may receive influences from both regions. However, the forces that comprise the soul's realm are not in any way subject to the forces of physical nature.

The sacred task of all human beings is to elevate their lower nature so that it serves that which is higher in them. Only in this way can mortal humans attain their eternal form and thereby come into being as individuated entities within the spiritual realm.

This is why we need also to transcend the realm of the soul and return to the Origin— our original Being as it was in the realm of Spirit which we had once left.

Only here are we truly "at home" and only from here are we able to preserve ourselves eternally.

Here the sublime spiritual community, from whose midst I speak to you, has its Temple and from here all who earnestly seek guidance, and demonstrate their sincerity though the way they live their lives, will receive it.

❧

Brothers in the Spirit are we, begotten of the eternal Spirit, united as one body and working among humanity since time immemorial. Only he can become our brother who has been prepared by the primordial Word before his birth onto the earthly plane—and then only after having been guided by us to spiritual maturity, so that he may perform his tasks on earth and, finally, be led into our midst to be one of us.

The foolhardy have in every age tried to reach us using clandestine paths. But they have always come up against an insurmountable barrier that does not allow them to so much as catch a glimpse of our Temple, even from afar. The timeless laws inherent in the realm of radiant Spirit cannot be circumvented by those who have the arrogance to believe that they can find the path to the Spirit without following the one and only path the Spirit *itself* has prepared since the dawn of time for all who seek its Light.

"No one cometh unto the Father, but by me." (John 14:6 KJV) These words were once spoken by one of us who had truly become "the way." But, alas, people did not understand his words and thought him to be a god who had taken on human form—an idea popular in the thinking of his time.

He answered them by saying: "Why callest thou me good? None is good, save one, that is, God." (Luke 18:19 KJV)

He truly was, however, a "son of God," begotten of the eternal Spirit. So also were his spiritual brothers and he did not conceal the truth that in his father's house there were "many mansions."*

---

* "In my Father's house are many mansions: if it were not so, I would have told you." (John 14:2 KJV) While the King James Version of the New Testament translates the original Greek as "mansions," newer translations substitute "rooms" or "dwellings"—more in keeping with the house analogy. Writing in German, Bô Yin Râ uses the word *Wohnungen*, which is closer in meaning to "dwelling." Bô Yin Râ uses this image to refer to the relationship between Jesus, his spiritual brothers and "the Father"—the human being of the Origin.

It is not he who is to blame for the teachings that have grown and entwined themselves around his name—doctrines that have grown out of ancient teachings about divinities, and which have made out of him a god in human form on this small planet.

ॐ

To be sure, the Light that illuminated his being was more intense than that of the Indian prince, known to the world as Gautama Buddha, for the Buddha embodied a human being who had *attained* the light of the Spirit but not one who had been *born* into the Light.

This Buddha had not himself become "the way," nor had he been prepared by the Spirit to become so. Only his boundless love for all living creatures enabled him to forge a path which leads to inner illumination. Yet his path does not lead to a true regaining of the state of oneness with the Spirit, even if some of its byways may lead there in time. These branchings off, however, are not the paths that the Buddha himself originally marked out, but follow quite different, more ancient guideposts.

In our time we tend to blur the differences which clearly distinguish the teachings of this sage from those of the Master of Nazareth, which are alive with the spiritual might that emanated from his being.

One must first learn to recognize who this Master really was—one who could say of himself: "I am the way, the truth, and the life..." (John 14:6 KJV)

One must first learn to understand why he was entitled to say: "He that is not with me is against me; and he that gathereth not with me scattereth abroad." (Matthew 12:30 KJV)

I am speaking here of the historical person referred to in the Gospels—not to the cult figure of adoration believed by its many faithful to be that same person.

Likewise I am speaking of the historical person referred to as Gautama Buddha who walked the lands of India as a teacher.

One must clearly separate these *human* personalities from the Being who dwells within the Godhead—the sublime *godly* Being—worshipped and adored in Northern Buddhism as the highest heavenly Buddha or Adi-Buddha and by the Christians as the Christ.

Theological confusion results from the failure to distinguish between a human mortal on this earth, however sublime, and the highest embodiment of primordial Light in the form of the most sublime individuated Being dwelling in the realm of *Spirit*. This confusion is the main reason why people do not understand who the Master of Nazareth truly was and why they are unable to grasp the true meaning of the Logos, which is "the Word that is God"—primordial Light expressing itself in individuated form within the realm of spirit.*

This aspect of the Spirit, expressing itself as the highest individuated Being, is the timeless point of origin for all the spiritual hierarchies, which then reach down to those few spiritually awakened beings on this earth who represent their end point. It is the beings who comprise the hierarchies of the Spirit who continually prepare a few, while they are still

---

* "In the beginning was the Word, and the Word was with God, and the Word was God." (John 1:1 KJV) "I am Om, the Word that is God." (Bhagavad Gita 7:8)

in the realm of the Spirit, to reestablish the union of the human spirit with this eternal point of origin. In theological doctrine, the distinction between the point of origin in the realm of Spirit and its end point on earth have been blurred—a source of confusion only very few have been able to recognize.

At the heights to which Gautama Buddha was able to climb, there is no longer a reason for prayer that can be justified by logic. Still, there is a far more exalted state that even the Buddha's highest ascent could not reach. This higher state cannot be scaled by effort, but can be reached only by flying on the Spirit's wings—and it is only in this state, united with God within the embrace of the radiant Spirit, that prayer truly becomes the expression of the most intimate union of the individuated, timeless human being with the Light of the Beginning from whence it has its life.

Only in this state can these words of the Master of Nazareth be fully understood: "Ask, and it shall be given you; seek, and ye shall find; knock, and it shall be opened unto you." (Matthew 7:7 KJV) And further: "…Whatsoever ye shall ask the Father in my name, he will give it you." (John 16:23 KJV)

However, he who promised eternal life to all who believed in him and lived according to his words knew only too well that for the full meaning of his teachings to be understood something more was needed than the comprehension that can be gained from "flesh and blood."

He speaks of those who are "outside"—those who are of this earthly world: "because they seeing see not; and hearing they hear not, neither do they understand." (Matthew 13:13 KJV)

But there will, at all times, be those who are "outside."

∞

THOSE WHO STILL STRIVE to master the occult forces of innermost nature, those who hold themselves out to be spiritual teachers without having the slightest knowledge as to where their supposed wisdom comes from, those who are still enveloped in deep darkness and yet wish to be seen as a light unto others, those who worship the mind and have made an idol out of thinking, those who try to circumvent the *one* path that leads into the Spirit, although it certainly would be open to them—to all

119

these we cannot send the help that the realm of Spirit has to offer, much as we may pity them in their delusion.

Those who in blind ignorance believe themselves to be safely sheltered within the realm of soul, without having mastered the forces of this realm, will also call in vain for spiritual help.

Only those who resolutely wrest themselves away from the occult forces of physical nature; those who have learned to master the forces of their soul and then strive yet higher to reach the realm of radiant Spirit, will be granted help from that realm—because only then can that help be received and put to use. Only to those the Spirit has commanded us to help may we bring the help that is available from the Spirit's sublime energies.

Those to whom we send our help will be liberated from all lower, base desires to dominate and within the realm of radiant Spirit—the home from whence they originated and which they had left eons ago—they will regain the consciousness that had once been theirs.

Having come alive again at last within the realm of radiant Spirit, their life shall be a life of love, for they will know that nothing can abide within the Spirit that is unworthy of love, and nothing can endure that can arouse their hatred.

※

ALREADY THOUSANDS OF YEARS AGO there were those who had lost their way and, knowing that they had forfeited their ability to develop spiritually, sought in vain to defame the spiritual community to which my words bear witness. But their attempts to sully us with their poisonous venom always fail for such foulness invariably falls back upon those who indulge in it.

With those of us who are alive in the realm of radiant Spirit but also living on earth in mortal bodies live those who are not fated to be mortals but, rather, dwell eternally on the spiritual plane. It is they who have been the targets of such vicious rage. But if one were now to search all of physical nature throughout the cosmos, or the realm of the soul and the realm of the radiant Spirit, not even a trace would be found of their foolish slanderers.

Nothing impure can attain eternal life within the realm of radiant Spirit.

"For without are dogs, and sorcerers, and whoremongers, and murderers, and idolaters, and whosoever loveth and maketh a lie." (Revelation 22:15 KJV)

"Blessed are they which are called unto the marriage supper of the Lamb." (Revelation 19:9 KJV)

The one who wrote these words two thousand years ago knew full well from whence he had received the call to write them. One should be aware, however, that very little of what has been attributed to him was actually written by him.

He spoke of the same things as others of his calling; the same things I now speak of using different images and language.

The spiritual community which revealed itself to him has at all times expressed itself in symbolism and language appropriate to time and place.

The forms in which this revelation occurs differ from religion to religion and among the various peoples of the world, but those who find their way to any one of these forms can rest assured that they stand on solid ground.

They are treading the path the Spirit has prepared for them—no matter what name they give it. In Islam too, in the very strict forms determined by the Quran, innermost revelations of the realm of radiant Spirit have been received time and again throughout the ages by worthy seekers, just as they have also been received by authentic Indian yogis or the initiates of ancient Greece.

※

CHAPTER FIVE

WHAT NEEDS TO BE UNDERSTOOD

ALL THE WORLD'S RELIGIONS CALL UPON human beings to turn back in some way—to search for and find again their original home within the Spirit—although each faith may envision this spiritual home and the path that leads there in very different ways.

Common to all religions, however, is the realization that the condition in which humans find themselves in their existence here on earth is not the same as what they may experience in their primordial home within the realm of Spirit. There is the realization as well that this renewed state of being can only be attained through ennoblement of one's actions; that is, by subordinating one's lower impulses to higher ones.

In almost all religions one finds traces of ancient truths about Reality: the understanding that the timeless Light of the Beginning may express itself in individualized form. In Taoism, Shintoism and the Hînayâna school of the Southern Buddhists, however, such a conception is not to be found. Nonetheless, it would be a mistake to label these religions as being "atheistic" even though their concepts concerning the divine do not rise above the formless, *unindividuated* sea of the eternal Ground of Being.

Northern Buddhism is known as the Mahâyâna school, or the "greater vehicle," in contrast to the "smaller vehicle," or Hînayâna school of Southern Buddhism. Mahâyâna Buddhism does have within it the concept of the timeless Light of the Origin expressed in individualized form; its purest representation is the primordial, heavenly Buddha known as Adi-Buddha. This concept may have its origins in Gnostic thought, reaching Nepal and Tibet only in much later times via Persia and Turkestan—although the clarity of the original insight has been blurred by different schools of thought.

The concept of the Logos has its origin in Gnostic insight as well. "The Word which is with God and which is God" (John 1:1 KJV) is nothing other than a description of the time-less, unfathomable Light of the Beginning expressing itself in an individualized, spiritual form. This insight into spiritual reality found its way into Christian dogma where it became intermingled with the very different, ancient concept of divine sonship. As a result of this confusion, the Christos of the Gospels—the Master of Nazareth, the "anointed one"—has now for some two thousand years been mistakenly considered to be and has been worshiped as an incarnation of Logos: "the Son of God."*

❧

IN ITS ESSENCE, the Alexandrian doctrine of the Logos reflects, with complete clarity,

---

* The Greek word Logos has been translated in English as "the Word." However, in most schools of Greek philosophy, the term was used to designate a rational, intelligent and vivifying principle of the universe. In early Jewish thought, the concept of the Word (*davar*) described God's wisdom, utterances and actions.

the knowledge of a Reality—and that Reality has been used as the basis for concepts of a personal god. The concept of a personal god remains rooted in Reality so long as it does not degenerate into an anthropomorphism that is not at all spiritual and which leads one to dream of a God above the clouds who is nothing more than an all-too-worldly potentate endowed with imaginary, divine powers.

Lamentably, the popular Christian understanding of God is not very far from such a view.

As a result, there are only two ways by which humans may approach this heavenly "king": Either one fears that one will not have his ear if one stands before him alone, without an advocate and, therefore—in imitation of the courtly practices of a bygone age—seeks the assistance of spiritual mediators; or one arrogantly disdains all assistance and feels entitled to speak directly to the heavenly king without the aid of mediation.

Both approaches are reflective of a narrow, earth-bound understanding of divine Being— even if worshippers believe they are experiencing God in a spiritual way.

The "God" one wishes to communicate with in either of these two ways is still always only a "dreamed-up" God, regardless of what the worshipper may experience.

How small-minded and, at the same time, how arrogant and presumptuous is the supposition that one can gain the favor of one's God through an advocate or that one might seek a personal dialogue with the primordial Light—that one may approach the eternal Ground of all Being by such means. The Light of the Origin and its timeless self-expression in an individuated form surpasses all human comprehension, just as the great, fiery orbs in the vastness of space outshine a tiny ember smoldering on a hearth.

❦

BUT FOR THE PATH PREPARED FOR US by the eternal, all-embracing Spirit emanating from the Light of the Beginning, not a single human spirit could ever find its way back to its timeless origin.

This path is the self-same path that the human spirit had once traversed before the "fall" in which it became incarnated in the human animal dwelling on this earth.

This path would be impassible if *all* human spirits had "fallen" simultaneously.

To be sure, only a small number of human spirits are ever fated to undergo this fall even if, over the course of millennia, these relatively few form myriads who are to share in the life of the animal kingdom during their time on this and other planets.

There are a few human spirits who were never destined to undergo a fall into the human animal but who have been living on this earth of their own free will since time began, in a form invisible to mortal eyes. Here they dwell, suffused with divine love and compassion, in order to keep the path that leads back to the Light of the Beginning open for their fallen brothers. They are guided in their sacred task by one of the primordial beings dwelling in the realm of radiant Spirit—abiding without cease in the Word of the Beginning, "the Word which is with God and which is God."

∞

SINCE TIME IMMEMORIAL these few spirits who dwell invisibly among us here on earth have been preparing those human spirits destined to be born into the human animal so that they, once born, can attain the hallowed state that enables them to become a bridge upon which their fellow, fallen human spirits can cross over to the headlands of that blessed realm of the transcendent Spirit from which they had been exiled.

These few who serve as bridges to the Spirit and who dwell here among us on this earth thus become Mediators of Primordial Light through the timeless essence with which they have become imbued. They may be referred to as the "elder brothers of humanity," to use a term that is in current usage. They are "older" because they would have been born millennia before their actual birth into mortal form had they not decided, of their own free will, to offer themselves to those brothers who have never fallen but are living here on earth in spiritual form, so that they may receive the necessary preparation, prior to their fall, to act as human "lenses" capable of collecting and concentrating rays of primordial Light.

This preparation cannot be complete without service for *millennia* to their never-fallen brothers abiding in love and compassion in spiritual form here on earth, so that those who are being prepared might aid in the task of liberation and illumination that they will perform during their sojourn on this earth in physical bodies. Thus, through their time of serving, those who are being prepared to act as mediators already had become helpers to human beings on earth long before their birth into the human animal.

Once born into a mortal human body, Mediators of Primordial Light are not all accorded the same task to accomplish during their time on earth.

Each is obligated to follow his own unique calling and will stay true to it alone, regardless of whether life on this earth will bring him wealth, position and honor or poverty, low estate, martyrdom, and contempt.

Were he to seek to elude the fate that life has in store for him, then he would fall far lower than ever before. It matters not whether the fate he wishes to escape is one most mortals seek or one they try to avoid. A Mediator cannot meet all the demands of his own unique calling unless he lives the sort of life wise guidance proffers to him—for it is a life especially suited to the task entrusted to him alone.

The community of those alive within the Spirit who are here on this earth in mortal form is united by the subtlest, immaterial bonds. It exerts a "magnetic" attraction, a purely spiritual energy that cannot be perceived by physical senses, to reach those other human beings who are able and ready to transcend their mortality and to be uplifted to a spiritual state which equals that of those who are part of this community. However, the human spirits who have been thus awakened are lifted to this level only so that they can continue on their path; they are neither obligated to nor capable of joining in the task of helping all humanity. That task is the ceaseless, sacred work of the Mediators of Primordial Light, as it requires a lengthy preparation lasting thousands of years before birth into a physical body.

Those who have awakened through the help of the community which the Spirit has ordained to this task will immediately, following their death, be able to ascend to the next, higher spiritual level, where those who have never fallen live in spiritual form. These never-fallen ones who live in *spiritual* form ceaselessly send their radiant energy to the community of pure spirits that lives here on earth in *mortal* form—the Mediators of Primordial Light—and it, in turn, ceaselessly receives those spiritual impulses. Without the help of these spiritual impulses, a mortal human never could become conscious of and manifest the Eternal so as to mediate timeless Light to others.

Among this community of mediators here on earth, there are a few who, after the mortal body that served them has died, and once they thereupon have attained this higher level, choose, out of overflowing love and compassion, to remain among humanity on earth in an invisible form. Through their presence on the earthly plane, and through the accumulation of power generated by their will, they support the never-fallen ones who dwell in the spiritual realm in their work of help and salvation for humanity.

Almost all of these mediators strive higher still, even after having reached the state in which the never-fallen ones dwell—with the exception of these few that Northern Buddhism refers to as "Bodhisattvas of Compassion," and the Christian church of earlier times calls its

"Saints," "Angels," and "Archangels"—including the "Fourteen Holy Helpers."* Thus the human spirit passes through each consecutively higher level of the spiritual hierarchy, over an immeasurably long period of time such that it cannot be comprehended by the human mind, until the primordial Being of the Origin—the expression of the Light of the Beginning in its individualized form—has at last been reached: this is "the Word which is with God and which is God." And now, united for all Eternity with this most sublime of all Beings, the human spirit—having already long ago reunited with its spiritual erotic polar opposite to form a male and female unity within the Spirit—finds its highest expression as a human being alive within the realm of Spirit.

In this way the fallen human spirit finds its way back from its incarnation as the mortal

---

* The Fourteen Holy Helpers are a group of saints venerated in Roman Catholicism because their intercession is believed to be particularly effective against disease. The origin of the Helpers dates back to the Black Death that devastated Europe in the mid-1300s.

creature of this earth to its primordial home within the realm of radiant Spirit.

Life in this world of bliss and clarity is completely different from anything to be found even in the most hidden regions of the physical universe, to which this earth belongs.

∾

THE PHYSICAL UNIVERSE is not very far removed from the realm of radiant Spirit or from the sea of the soul forces that provide the elements that make it possible for the human spirit to assume its individualized form. Nevertheless, there is a great divide that separates the world of matter from the world of radiant Spirit; a divide that could never be crossed had not those never-fallen ones who, abiding in spiritual form yet choosing to remain among the fallen human spirits, formed and maintained the only bridge across which a return to life within the timeless Spirit is possible.

Only after it returns to the Origin and is thus united with "the Word which is God"— through direct experience and not through an outer source—will the human spirit come face-to-face with the Godhead as it eternally *is* and carries out its purpose.

Only then will the human spirit apprehend all things as they truly are and only then will the human spirit be embraced by the Origin that is its home.

❧

THE JOURNEY OF THE HUMAN SPIRIT is immeasurably long but even from the first steps on the path the Living God can be born within.

The Living God of the awakening or awakened human being on this earth is a spark—unfathomable to the mortal mind—a scintilla of light issuing from the ever-radiant source of timeless Light which is the "Word" that is forever with "God." It is the primordial Light of the Beginning in its expression as primordial Word just as it also, at the same time, knows itself as timeless Godhead.

So that I might clear up any remaining misunderstanding, let me make a comparison with one of the forces of the physical universe that human beings have learned to master:

Electricity can cause a filament the thickness of a single hair to glow and give off light, yet that same electrical current, when magnified to the immense power needed to light a city, would instantly destroy this carbon filament. So, too, would the human mind be instantly destroyed if it were to approach the timeless Word in its full radiance—the Light of the Beginning itself—without the necessary preparation. Yet the human mind can easily bear the infinitely gentle current that within the most profound depths of the soul will produce a reflection of the Father: that luminous star through which one's Living God can be perceived even while here on earth, without one's mortal consciousness being destroyed by coming face-to-face with the full splendor of its radiance.

When at last awakened individuals pursue the one and only path that leads back to their primordial home within the Spirit, this guiding star will light the way and will shine ever more brightly as each higher state is reached. And now at last, within the indescribable splendor of the timeless Word of the Beginning, which dwells within the timeless Light of the Beginning that eternally gives birth to itself, awakened individuals finally unite with their guiding star for all Eternity.

This is a description of the path which leads the fallen human spirit upwards once again, insofar as it can be put into words.

This is what needs to be understood if one would find the only true path that leads into the living Spirit, and which is open to human beings. This is the path that all religions on this earth which draw their nourishment from the wellspring of the Spirit's realm believe exists, and try to guide their faithful towards, each in its own way.

Those who think they can reveal different paths to the Spirit deceive themselves. Even if they honestly believe they are acting with the best intentions, they will, nevertheless, lead themselves and all those who follow them towards inner confusion and torment— already here on earth and for eons following their mortal death. The end result could even be a complete disintegration of consciousness—an eternal, spiritual death from which there can be no resurrection.

The laws of the eternal, spiritual realm are unyielding and no power or wisdom on heaven or earth can bend them. They are the expression of the *will* of primordial Light itself—from which all things that *are* emanate.

❧

As you gaze upon the stars that fill the night sky you cannot fathom what sustains them, yet this entire universe with its countless solar systems is but the smallest testimony to a power and its inherent will to which you, too, owe your existence. And if you will pursue the path that love and compassion has made passible for you, even higher manifestations of this power—even its very *essence*—could reveal themselves to you.

But as it is written: "Eye hath not seen, nor ear heard, neither have entered into the heart of man, the things which God hath prepared for them that love him." (1 Corinthians 2:9 KJV) That is to say, nothing that is mortal can truly comprehend that which is eternal.

May my words lead you to love all that is divine.

Only when you come to recognize the divine, as far as you are able through inner contemplation, will you also be able to feel authentic love for it. Otherwise you will merely love a fetish you have created in your own mind.

Only when, in the stillness of your meditations, you can feel the force of the divine drawing you upward will you also be able to feel *within yourself* the timeless love through which you shall be able to accomplish all you need for your spiritual salvation.

Only then will you learn to use this force that has no equal and which masters every other force: the power of Love that needs no object.

This is the living, divine, primal *force of all forces,* and only through its power can the life of every human being on this earth be freed from bondage.

This highest of all forces can be the means to liberate yourself from the bonds by which the unseen powers of the physical cosmos, where you too live, hold you captive. These invisible powers are far below you in the hierarchy of all that is and yet, at this time, still more powerful than you—until the supreme power of Love that needs no object turns you from their prisoner into the invincible master of your life.

Then you will understand what these words mean: "God is love; and he that dwelleth in love dwelleth in God, and God in him." (1 John 4:16 KJV)

॰९

CHAPTER SIX

THE MYSTERY OF ARTISTIC EXPRESSION

THERE WAS A TIME WHEN BODY AND SOUL were viewed as different aspects of the human being, to be treated as separate from each other. People who counted themselves as being among those striving towards the Spirit felt ashamed to be burdened with a physical body—and perhaps many still think and feel this way.

The ones who remembered their soul came close to believing that they no longer needed their bodies. At best, they regarded the body as a leaden weight that might drag down the soul or perhaps as a necessary evil—an obstacle to the unfolding of the spirit, worthy only of contempt.

They believed they must mortify the body so as to liberate the soul. They did not understand that the soul reveals itself to human beings *through* the body: the soul's experience is conveyed to mortal consciousness through the body's awareness. Without the body the soul would be a yawning void, a speaking with no meaning, a clock without a face, a factory with a thousand whirring wheels producing nothing, a storehouse of riches that can never be retrieved.

We cannot conceive of or comprehend a single thought unless there exists within the body a corresponding physical analogue to that thought; a space in which the content of this thought is, as it were, represented in a manner that can be perceived by our mortal senses. Every mental image, even the most complex, is already represented by a form within the body and each sensation can only reach our conscious mind through the sense organs of the body.

Even in our day only a few know that something more than just the brain must be involved if those things the soul perceives are to reach our mortal consciousness. So long as we live in the material world and are fettered to the body, every atom of our body must stand in service to the soul. The riches of the soul are only accessible to us here on earth when body and soul work *together*.

What we call "feeling" and "sensing" is in a certain manner a manifestation of the same energy through which we are also able to think. Our ability to feel and sense can be refined to the same degree of sharpness as our thinking, if not more so—and most assuredly, to a much higher level of *certitude* than can be achieved through thinking.

The processes involved when we use these faculties can be likened to a sending forth of conscious and half-conscious questions at lightning speed, to which an answer usually follows with equal speed. These answers always come to us from the body, although we may not be aware of this—even if we think we can do without the body and look upon it with contempt.

For every thought we have, for every stimulus to the senses we receive—no matter how abstract the thought or how sublime or subtle the sensation—we simultaneously, with the use of our brain, send out a seeking impulse to those parts of our body in which an analog of that thought or that sensation exists in physical form. In almost the same instant, this impulse returns to report its findings—once again via the workings of the brain. It is not necessary for us to know where in the body that analog is located.

It is not easy to understand this process. Nevertheless, it is true that our perception of the physical world can only occur in this way. The entire external world would be nothing but chaos to us—a world without dimension or boundaries—and would be totally incomprehensible to the soul without the participation of the entire body. Not just the brain is involved, although the brain is the executive "hub" that governs the body and nothing the soul perceives can reach our consciousness without having first passed through this governing center, so that it may receive a form that can be comprehended by the soul.

❧

ARTISTIC INSPIRATION that arises from the soul can only reach us through the participation of the body.

Artistic expression becomes a language of the soul only if, consciously or unconsciously, the rhythms embedded in it *resonate* with analogous rhythms within the body.

In the visual arts, even the depiction of the human form and the setting in which the artist has placed it can only be received by the soul if it activates certain points of consciousness within the body that relate to the art being viewed. This is true even if viewers believe they are using only the eyes and the brain to absorb what they are seeing and experiencing.

Whoever approaches a work of art with the desire to experience its essence must rely on the body and will apprehend more through the body than they can know or might like to admit.

It is true that we hear music primarily through the ear, but the process of becoming conscious of it is far more complicated than most listeners suspect. The ear is merely the organ that receives the incoming sound waves. In order for the listener to make sense of them, those sound waves must be sent throughout the entire body until they find those places analogous to them: places that exhibit in analog form the same tonal intervals and the same relationship among the intervals as the music itself; the same vibrations and the same rhythms. In this way, like an echo, a response returns to the ear and is immediately transmitted to the brain and transformed into a language that can recognized by the soul.

The same happens with regard to the eye when the appreciation of architecture, sculpture, or painting is concerned. Where poetry is concerned, hearing is especially important, even if the poetry is read to oneself in silence. Indeed, often all the senses are in use at the same time.

The process is always the same.

"Mysterious even in the light of day..."*

Art is essentially a magic of symbols. The artist must find those symbols that will elicit from corresponding points within the body of the beholder the resonant *energy* that will allow the beholder to feel what the artist is intending to evoke.

---

* "Mysterious in the light of day, nature retains her veil, despite our clamours: that which she does not willingly display cannot be wrenched from her with levers, screws and hammers." This quote from Goethe's *Faust* (Part 1) would have been familiar to educated Europeans in Bô Yin Râ's day.

This resonance between artist and beholder, through the use of symbols that speak to the soul, is essential for both the creation and the appreciation of a work of art—even though the magic of artistic expression remains a mystery for creator and beholder alike.

⧽⧼

CHAPTER SEVEN

KABBALAH

THOSE FEW WHO ARE TRUE STUDENTS OF the Kabbalah, as well as countless would-be ones who have happened upon this book through the direction of those who hold the reins of the Chariot of Fire,* should not suppose that a secret manuscript of ancient Hebrew mysticism will be brought to light in these pages. I include here also those who presumptuously refer to themselves as Kabbalists while, ironically, often harboring anti-Semitic sentiments. I would refer the newcomer, who scarcely has any concept of what the Kabbalah is about, to the Kabbalah itself, available in translation in every major

---

* Bô Yin Râ is no doubt referring to Ezekiel's vision of the chariot, described in Ezekiel 1, which serves as a foundation for much of Kabbalistic literature and has been commented on extensively in Jewish exegesis for over two thousand years.

language, in order to better understand what this chapter is about. Of course, it is not necessary for readers to explore this area if they are not especially drawn to it.

I am not in a position to delve into the details of the various foundational Hebrew texts whose inner strength nourishes Orthodox Eastern European Judaism*—nor is there any reason I should do so, since there is much erudite commentary already available to the interested reader.

Instead, I will turn to the forgotten, original non-Jewish sources on which these Hebrew texts are based—sources of which I possess certain knowledge—and draw from their depths in order to illuminate what is most profound and essential in Kabbalistic wisdom.

༄

IN ORDER TO LAY a proper foundation for this discussion, and at the risk of offending those of Jewish blood who study the Kabbalah, I

---

* This article was written sometime before 1936, the publication date of the original German edition of this book. It predates the Holocaust, in which Eastern European Jewry was annihilated in the Nazi genocide.

am compelled—quite against my will—to conclude that the entire mystical system of Kabbalah is actually of non-Jewish origin. Rather, it has its roots in an esoteric body of teachings that can be traced back to the earliest sources of wisdom in India. Even today, the adherents of these teachings practice Kabbalah in their own way without having any knowledge of the Jewish Kabbalah or even so much as knowing its name.

I do not intend to go into further detail here but the truly knowledgeable Kabbalist will hardly disagree with me after having calmly and without prejudice finished this entire essay—while also reading between the lines. Those who are new to this subject may want to trust my guidance until they too shall be in a position to verify my conclusions.

These words are only meant to affirm the deep truths of the Kabbalah. However, those who revere the Kabbalah may forgive me if I here deal only with the fundamental principles of the whole system so that their great worth may be appreciated by my readers. I will not engage in polemics and try to dispute the popular thinking that attempts to create an aura of mystery around the Kabbalah, and is then deemed sacred and given honor it does not deserve. True Kabbalah can never be a matter for the common masses but, rather, will always remain an esoteric teaching for the very few.

This brief clarification is primarily intended to allow those who today still intuitively understand the genuine core of the ancient teachings to deepen their study of Kabbalah. But it is also my purpose to teach those less acquainted with the Kabbalah that this source of profound wisdom, which has come down to us in the Western world from the Far East through the form it took in medieval Jewish mysticism, is worthy of greatest respect. The wisdom of the Kabbalah has challenged the most outstanding minds of the Middle Ages and the Renaissance but its worth has only been recognized by a few—while many have actually ridiculed it, out of their own stupidity and arrogance. Notwithstanding, Kabbalah is still alive today but only a select few individuals—especially in Northern European countries—recognize that it deserves to be held with great reverence and is worthy of a life of painstaking study.

୬

THE ULTIMATE GOAL of the Kabbalah, as with all mysticism that is meant to be applied to everyday life, is to lead one back to the highest emanation of the Spirit from whence all life originates—to unite the soul with the Source of Life that it had once abandoned. This is the *unio mystica*: the fusion of the lone individual with the timeless, *primordial individual*—the wellspring that is the common ground of Being of all individual existence.

As part of their journey towards this goal, true students of Kabbalah engage in the magical practice of mastering certain energies that can influence this world of phenomena—an ability they have acquired as a result of living a life immersed in Kabbalistic discipline. They do not pursue this ability as an end in itself; it comes about, rather, of its own accord, once the student has entered into the hallowed state of *unio mystica*.

The Kabbalistic system is essentially a most venerable variation of the Yogic training rooted in the traditions of India.

❦

THIS SPECIAL YOGIC PRACTICE, known in the Western world in its hebraicized form as "Kabbalah," is still today devotedly pursued, just as it was thousands of years ago, in a few places in Central Asia—although no "globe-trotter" shall ever learn of it. Even a sojourn of decades in India will not earn a European enough spiritual credit with those who reside there and are knowledgeable about this practice to be allowed even the slightest insight into their carefully guarded mystical knowledge—unattainable even by most scholars. Nevertheless, not a single night passes during which a magical practice based on this is not performed, in a solemn, ceremonial way, in temples carefully protected from all desecration.

It hardly seems necessary to emphasize that these Indian, Tibetan, and Chinese "Kabbalists" are in dedicated spiritual contact with the sublime spiritual community of which I am a part. It is by virtue of my participation in this community that I have learned about these sacred things that have hardly ever before been revealed to a European—even Europeans who are familiar with all the countries mentioned here and fluent in their languages.

❧

When I speak here of this magic that is common to East and West, one should be mindful of the fact that the medieval Jewish Kabbalah represents a kind of translation and refashioning of the original "Kabbalah" which is its source. This original "Kabbalah" is still alive in the heart of Asia today and, although it bears a different name and uses different language to describe its principles, is identical in its essence with the Jewish Kabbalah. Using different wording, the book describes the principles that bring this pure Yoga practice— accessible only to a vanishing few—alive for the practitioner. Those rare, true Western Kabbalists who come across this book will quickly understand why I expressly point out the Indian origin of the Jewish Kabbalah.

When I speak of Kabbalah I certainly do not mean the kind of superstitious pseudo-magic practiced in major European and American cities by a few pathetic, stunted individuals who have usurped the name "Kabbalah" with brazen irresponsibility. Rather, I refer to the most profound spiritual wisdom as it may still occasionally be found among Eastern European Orthodox Jewry.* Non-Jewish pseudo-Kabbalists, who are far removed from Jewish spirituality, believe they are freebooters of Jewish wisdom and are pursuing Kabbalah with their foolish incantations—but in fact they have only created an absurd caricature of the true Kabbalah.

The awe-inspiring, enlightened Jews of medieval times and those Orthodox Jews who followed afterwards were zealous in their efforts to protect the esoteric knowledge of the Kabbalah, which they believed to have originated with their own people, from mere speculation and the magical superstitions that were rampant in the popular imagination of the time. They could hardly imagine that after a few hundred years there would be many extreme anti-Semites, ignorant of Hebrew and without the slightest feeling for Jewish piety, who would misuse Kabbalistic language and thought—often known to them only through highly questionable translations—for their

---

* See footnote on page 158. It should also be noted that the Kabbalah has nourished and continues to nourish Jewish communities in other parts of the world.

own magical doings, with no understanding of Jewish feeling and thought.

At the same time, I must emphatically caution against the widespread tendency to idolize everything related to the Kabbalah. I refer especially to the foolish notion that one should know of these things or risk being considered an ignoramus who lacks the capacity to appreciate a secret knowledge, the study of which many have considered to be their noblest task in life. As I have said, one needs to dedicate a lifetime to the study of Kabbalah in order to truly fathom the highest insights concealed in the deliberately ambiguous text and ornate images within its pages. A superficial, casual reading will merely lead to a deplorable occultism fed by tawdry little tracts written by irresponsible purveyors of Kabbalistic wisdom.

❧

CHAPTER EIGHT

THE LIGHT
OF THE SPIRIT
IN CHRISTIANITY

IN ALL THE GREAT RELIGIONS THAT HAVE been given to the world by enlightened individuals throughout time, scintillas of the Spirit's light still glimmer. It is not my intention, however, to examine these religions here and point out every instance where true insight into matters of the Spirit is expressed. One would have to write lengthy tomes to do justice to their most important teachings and to the lives of their most illustrious faithful.

Let us focus here solely on Christianity, which many consider to be the only true religion, many more merely respect and still others hate and attack. Be that as it may, Christianity is unquestionably the religion that is most familiar and relevant to those who live in the Western hemisphere.

But even as I write this, I can already hear my readers ask the question: To which version of Christianity might I be referring? Those who adhere to older systems such as Greek Orthodox or Roman Catholicism consider their own form of faith to be the only correct one, just as those who follow one of the countless younger denominations are disposed to see only foolish superstition in the older ones. The hatred between Christians of differing denominations is a far greater enemy of Christianity than all the corrosive criticism and ridicule leveled by those who spurn its teachings.

Unspeakable harm has befallen individuals and nations because of differing opinions and conflicts about articles of faith—and still there is no end to this evil that is stirred up constantly in the name of Christian faith.

But the objections raised against Christianity by individuals with superficial insight into it have little to do with the essence of Christianity itself.

Their attacks are a product of narrow-mindedness, prejudice, and dogmatism. They spring from a misguided, all-too-human quest for power: the compulsive need to dominate others and control even the most private depths of their being and—not lastly—the delusion that one is possessed of the only "truth" and must impose it on others, even against their will, so that their souls might be "saved."

I do not wish, however, to focus on these distortions of true Christian faith which are, unfortunately, so commonly engaged in by misguided Christians.

Everyone is aware that even the most bizarre beliefs held by certain Christians will find zealous defenders who claim to be filled with genuine religious fervor.

❦

CHRISTIANITY HAS EMERGED only recently on this earth, and is still too young for its profound, spiritual depths to be fully understood. Those who believe it has outlived itself and has become irrelevant because of the sins of its churches are quite mistaken. They only consider the manner in which Christianity has been practiced up until now and do not have the foresight to realize that a time will come when almost everything that is considered "Christianity" today will be looked back upon with shame—just as mature adults often look back at the arrogant demands and follies of their youth with embarrassment.

I would caution the reader, however, to not misinterpret my words.

I do not mean to imply that until now *nothing* of true Christianity may be found in the world. Nevertheless, I must not neglect to point out that for most of those who have called and today call themselves "Christians," the true core of Christianity still lies hidden, covered over like delicious fruit ripening within a thick, hard shell. One has yet to savor the sweetness of its innermost core, even if some of its nectar has seeped through the shell, so that one may drink in its fragrance.

As yet no one knows, and many do not wish to know, what can be found by penetrating this innermost core of Christianity: the Reality that is pure, radiant Spirit. Before one can free the divine core of Christianity and behold its inner mystery, one must first recognize that the husks that cover this core are nonessential. Only then shall it be possible to build a tabernacle that will house this radiant core so that humanity may see and honor it and, for all time to come, worship it in forms worthy of its essence.

❦

Pious Christian souls will no doubt feel uplifted when familiar details of Christianity's beginnings are commemorated. However, in doing so, one forgets that the seed is something other than the sprout, and the sprout different from the maturing plant, which in turn is different from the blossom and the blossom something other than the mature fruit.

Anyone who tries to continuously prune a young plant will restrict its development and keep it from unfolding naturally; it will not be allowed to mature and grow beyond the size and shape it had as a sprout. Such a person would surely not be considered a good gardener.

As of this time, Christianity may be compared to a plant that is still unfolding. It is not the task of Christianity's faithful followers to cut off each and every shoot at the rootstock because it appears to them that the plant is growing too luxuriantly; rather, they should allow the plant to grow and freely unfold in all its abundance. None of its shoots and branches should be stopped from following their natural course of development, so long as they draw their nourishment from the plant's roots, and even though they appropriate the life-giving energy of the soil for themselves—and thus diminish it for the others.

Pruning efforts are quite inappropriate here because the plant cannot grow by absorbing nourishment from its own center. It must assimilate substances from outside itself, transform them and thus make them part of itself.

The first leaves that sprout around the bud in such abundance wither away completely once they have completed their task of sheltering the sprouting shoot, and new branches and leaves take their place. This new growth is destined to become part of the mature plant and will take on the features of the plant's unique character, while the early growth falls into oblivion and is forgotten.

❧

THE "PLANT" KNOWN as Christianity has been pruned and trimmed to excess. With the best of intentions, people have tried to shape it and control its growth, so it is no wonder that the plant has been held back from developing naturally.

One might consider it a miracle that this plant is still alive, despite all the harsh treatment it has received.

It is best to refrain from disturbing the life-giving sap of Christianity or attempting to control the growth of the "plant." Instead, one should appreciate the multiplicity of all its older and newer shoots, leaving the plant's growth in the hands of the Eternal Gardener, who knows what is good for it. In due time the excess shoots will disappear and the healthy sprouts will fulfill their destiny and grow into their most magnificent beauty.

❧

I HOPE THE READER will forgive me for speaking in metaphors, but through the use of metaphor those willing to understand me will be able to decipher what I have to say without my being compelled to offend pious souls belonging to any particular denomination of Christian faith.

I do not favor any one of the Christian forms of faith over the other. I see in each of them the workings of divine spiritual force. This despite the fact that they are each impeded in their development by well-intended but narrow-minded beliefs, fear of having to surrender cherished articles of faith, or fear of having to reclaim past religious tenets that were once thought to be unacceptable.

One should also bear in mind that everything rooted in eternal Truth can manifest in a multitude of forms.

The time has come for humanity to awaken to full consciousness of the timeless core of Christianity while also remaining tolerant and respectful of the differences in practice among its adherents.

To use yet another metaphor, the needs of the eagle differ from those of the nightingale, but every living being on this earth breathes the same life-giving air. Similarly, the needs of the human soul vary greatly from person to person, yet all require nourishment from the same divine Light of the Spirit if they are to live and thrive.

❧

In Christianity, the most profound spiritual forces are at work, despite all the human shortcomings I have described and even despite the atrocities that have been committed in its name. It is hard to understand why its faithful followers honor this religion above all others, given the way it has been shaped by history and has been practiced to the present day—yet their devotion is in fact a testament to the eternal wellspring of spiritual energies from which it still draws its nourishment.

Ancient wisdom, rooted in the source of life that is Eternity, is concealed in its articles of faith—the full meaning of which is seldom recognized and hardly perceived by the vast majority of believers.

Much of what was once incorporated into Christian doctrine by those who were suffused with the Spirit's light was later expunged by those who held more narrow, puritanical views and who could not reconcile this enlightened Christianity with their dogmatic understanding of the faith. In today's deadening climate of spiritual emptiness, most still cannot see these bright reflections of eternal Truth, and regard them instead as mere remnants of pagan superstition.

Enlightened individuals who had been initiated into those ancient mysteries in which a knowledge of eternal Reality was still alive have erected the temple to these teachings that is Christianity, guided by the clear vision of their spiritual insight. No matter how well-intentioned the motives of those who came after and took offense at the design of this temple, they did not have the same depth of insight as those who once laid its foundation and created its structure.

Although their criticisms were indeed justified and their intentions innocent, they desecrated this temple, with no understanding of what they were doing. When we examine the history of Christianity over time, we see all too clearly that essential building blocks have been removed and, without these supports, the masonry has been slowly and unavoidably crumbling.

Despite all this, Christianity will fulfill its destiny: to become a living reflection of the timeless mysteries and to give them shape and form on earth. Only a renewed, deep delving into these mysteries can bring a halt to the aborted unfolding of this destiny, inspire mutual understanding and tolerance among the various Christian denominations and usher in a new era of cross-fertilization and flowering.

༜

OPPOSING POINTS OF VIEW should be allowed to coexist as long as they still serve a purpose and no one should presume to sit in judgment of them; only those high powers who shape the spiritual development of humanity on earth are capable of uniting the opposites, and at the appropriate time.

The true helpers of Christianity today are, above all, those Germans who are commonly referred to as "medieval mystics." They are the *true* theosophists in the Paulinian sense of the word: those who knew the Reality of the Spirit and who, in their writings, brought tidings of its radiant realm to all. I refer to such enlightened individuals as Eckhart, Tauler, and the Master of the Teutonic Order of Frankfurt whose name is not known and to whom we owe the *Book of the Perfect Life*, also referred to as the *Theologia Deutsch*. Also included are the canon Thomas à Kempis, who wrote *The Imitation of Christ* and, for those who do not feel overwhelmed by his grand cosmic visions, Jacob Boehme, the seer of Görlitz. Angelus Silesius, although primarily a poet, should also not be forgotten here.

༄

ALL THIS OPENS UP spacious, far-reaching vistas within which a new kind of theology can be envisioned—a newer theology without whose purposeful help the damage done thus far cannot be healed.

The most important task of this new theology will be to untangle the dogmatic confusion that has resulted from equating the Master of Nazareth with the Logos—primordial Light as it expresses itself as the Word—a confusion that is the result of a limited, mortal perspective and has been reinforced throughout the history of the Christian religion.

A true "Re-formation," a thorough clarification and reformulation of concepts, is desperately needed here.

One needs a clear description of the Logos— the Godhead expressing itself as the eternal Word which is with God and which is

God—that is distinct from an understanding of the full potential of what a human being can attain in union with the Spirit, as embodied in the Master of the Gospels. Such an effort should be grounded in theology so that older dogmas are not superseded but, rather, are *transfigured*. This undertaking awaits the person who possesses the courage, knowledge, insight and position needed to make it possible—and the blessings that could flow from it would truly be immeasurable.

The ancient wisdom that I am obliged to proclaim in our day in no way contradicts the eternal core of Christianity, as much as it may appear so at first glance.

Anyone who understands from which source my teachings spring will find even the thought that any sort of contradiction could exist to be absurd.

At the same time, it is not my task to be an advocate for any sort of religious system that humanity has created, not even the sublime edifice of teachings that is Christianity.

My only obligation is to make evident to all the sacred, timeless values that have fertilized this world's great religions and to which *every* great religious system on this earth bears witness.

This does not prevent me, however, from making my own, personal contribution to a genuine deepening of Christian life based on my unique, inner knowledge—especially since I was born into a family whose German Christian lineage dates back many generations and I grew up being instructed in the Christian faith.

My teachings have already guided a growing number of believers, including pastors of the two principal Christian denominations, on their searching journeys through the wondrous world of Christian dogma. I have no reason to doubt that ever more individuals of good intent will embrace what I have written, often using different words that speak to their own Christian idiom, so that they may absorb it and find in it solid support for their faith.

႙

IT IS NOT NECESSARY and, indeed, would be highly detrimental, to want to establish new Christian or other spiritual communities.

We certainly have more than enough church denominations and other Christian sects.

All those, however, who feel at home in *any* of these congregations, and hold the inner conviction that the Christian form of worship speaks more to their heart than any other, should in their own way put their life in the service of the timeless, divine spiritual core of Christianity, so that through their own deepening understanding and faith it might be more and more made manifest to all humanity.

They should also try to understand others whose journeys to touch the living core of Christianity take a form different from their own and learn to respect the guidance these others receive from the Spirit.

They must stay far away from that pharisaic sort of self-righteousness in which reverence for Christian dogma is perversely expressed as intolerance of and even hatred for those who seek the truth in non-Christian forms.

Even at this time, there are men living in remote regions of central Asia who possess genuine insight into the essence of Christianity—beyond the understanding of any European, excepting the one speaking here. And yet, not one of them would even think of joining a group professing the Christian faith.

"And I say unto you, That many shall come from the east and west, and shall sit down with Abraham, and Isaac, and Jacob, in the kingdom of heaven." (Matthew 8:11 KJV)

Only foolish arrogance and blind insolence would dare predict the intentions of the divine Spirit regarding the future of Christianity.

The Lord of the harvest has sent laborers into his vineyard everywhere and every fruitful vine shall be carefully tended to by them.[*]

The radiant sun of the Spirit shall ripen the fruits of all the vines at such time as the Spirit deems appropriate.

∝

---

[*] The imagery in this sentence is based on Luke 10:2: "Therefore said he unto them, The harvest truly is great, but the labourers are few: pray ye therefore the Lord of the harvest, that he would send forth labourers into his harvest."

CHAPTER NINE

THE SECRET OF THE ANCIENT LODGES

I WILL NOW SPEAK OF THE SPIRITUAL lodges that have at all times sought workers willing to assist in the construction of the sublime spiritual Temple of God. Only the Mediators of Primordial Light living on this earth, who are far removed from personal ambition and from any desire for power and who act solely in the service of that which is *eternal* in humankind, know the blueprints and dimensions of this Temple. All human beings can become workers and assist in the construction of this living cathedral if they are willing to diligently work to develop the eternal in themselves, so that they come to embody the highest spiritual form that is the fulfillment of their innate potential.

Since earliest times on earth, those who were ready to receive the teachings and do the necessary inner work came together in associations, often governed by rather curious regulations. Although the myths that have been passed down about the history of these associations may seem like no more than fairy tales, they come much closer to the truth regarding the origin of these strivings—which date as far back as the time of the first mortal creatures who had become *human beings* in the true sense of that word—than what modern research can unearth, as such intellectual efforts are based on information that comes to us only from rather late chroniclers.

The temples of ancient Egypt were built to serve the development of the soul by those knowledgeable about that which is eternal in the mortal, human being. The same is true of the Parthenon and of many famous cathedrals built during the Christian era, as well as the architectural masterpieces of the ancient and medieval Orient and the work of the master builders of ancient Mexico. All these temples reveal in visible form energies that speak to the soul—through symbols taken from the timeless Temple that cannot be seen by mortal eyes and from which the impulse to build for the sake of the soul's development emanates.

These symbols are visual representations of invisible, spiritual realities—too sacred to be described in spoken language. The master architects of ancient times had themselves created this symbolic language: These master builders were pupils of those who are enlightened masters of the invisible architecture of the timeless Temple and its ornamentation—the Mediators of Eternal Light—and, even to this day, countless buildings and ruins bear witness to this truth.

જી

THE IMPULSE that has moved individuals to help one another in their inner development and the many different names under which they joined together to work towards that goal originate from different sources and should not be confused with one another. The names have changed over time but the commitment to the task of leading one another to God has always remained the same.

To be sure, one should not believe that one might ever find an individual who has attained spiritual *perfection* and is possessed of truly profound knowledge of the Eternal in any of these spiritually oriented lodges.

Nowadays these lodges, whose members once engaged in spiritual work together, are at best merely repositories of the tools, plans, and templates needed for this work—storehouses for ancient, sacred symbols whose correct interpretation enables the initiate to truly begin to absorb the teachings. At present, however, those coming together for mutual learning are not able—or do not dare—to interpret such sacred symbols and grasp their full power, except in a philistine manner; that is, according to rational understanding, or even in a fantastical way.

Despite all this, each lodge where once the divine was sought remains a sacred place and *nothing* in it shall ever be lost that is being preserved—albeit unknowingly—and is waiting there quietly for a later time. This is true even if members themselves, fearing persecution, sometimes destroy objects which hold symbolic meaning lest their activities be discovered, and it is true even if today's custodians only respect out of a sense of piety what they no longer know how to use for the development of their own timeless, inner self.

When the time is ripe, enlightened builders will again arise who will know how to use the implements preserved in these lodges. They will be grateful to those who are today the guardians of these sources of sacred wisdom for keeping them intact and not allowing them to be dispersed, even though they no longer understand their value.

∽

IT IS POSSIBLE that these new, enlightened builders will continue to use the same name as their predecessors and pass it down through the generations, but this is not a necessary condition for the work of "construction" on each member's spiritual dimension. The name that a particular group may have chosen, or even the misuse of a name, has nothing to do with the essence of the matter—not today and not even in earlier generations.

Nor is it absolutely necessary for a true "stonemason" who is guided by the Spirit and contributing to the construction of the Temple of the Spirit on earth to belong to such a working group. Some prefer to work only under the direct guidance of the Mediators of Primordial Light, who are the keepers of the blueprints for this divine edifice, and will only join a lodge when once again they can find those among its members who know how to use the tools that are stored there.

⚮

So what exactly is meant by "spiritual implements," "spiritual stonemasonry," and "construction of the Temple in the realm of Spirit?"

As a way of fostering better understanding of the highest art—the art of developing one's spiritual organism—let me attempt to provide an answer to all those ready to receive it.

I will do this without divulging secrets of this art that can only be mastered through struggle and without betraying the sanctity of mysteries embedded in the blueprints of the Temple—mysteries which can only be comprehended by those who have been sanctified to approach them. I will here be mindful of the words: "Give not that which is holy unto the dogs, neither cast ye your pearls before swine...." (Matthew 7:6 KJV) Christian communities and also non-Christian communities of antiquity and the Orient imposed the most severe punishment on any who ignored such advice.

☙

EACH OF THOSE who participates in the construction of this most sublime of all cathedrals—a cathedral of the Spirit—is at once worker, implement and stone.

One becomes a *worker* through one's own free will and is transformed into an *implement* by having practiced and learned the art of interpreting the sacred symbols and thus understanding how they are to be applied. Lastly, through this freely-chosen inner work and by applying the implement one has become in the way it must be used, one shapes oneself into a *stone,* now perfected so that it can be used in the construction of the cathedral.

The cathedral of humanity, constructed in accordance with the blueprints given by divine Love which is *God,* can only come into being when the stones that are needed to build it are skillfully hewn, under the spiritual guidance of the supervising stonemasons.

All those who assist as best they can in the construction of this most sacred Temple of God aspire to transform themselves into stones worthy of being incorporated into the Temple's structure. In this work, they follow the directions of those who, through their own will, have been hewn into towering columns, the monoliths that support the vaulted ceilings and the great dome of the Temple.

All those who would transform themselves into a stone that can be used in the construction of the Temple must study the craft of stonemasonry and take instruction from one who has mastered it. In this way they will learn how to use the implements of this craft to shape themselves in accordance with the guidelines given by the Spirit.

They are as yet rough, irregularly shaped stones, just freshly mined from the quarry. They must, through their own efforts, chisel and polish themselves so that they may fit perfectly into that place in the Temple's structure which is reserved for them alone.

Once transformed, they will willingly allow themselves to be fitted, each into their destined place, in the sacred Temple of the Spirit.

※

However, their task is still not completed.

As yet, they are dark within—but they must become *luminous*. The cathedral that is being built must be constructed of stones that are illuminated from within so that it may radiate light throughout the vastness of eternal space.

The ancient, sacred symbols of the spiritual lodges, to which initiates were introduced at the beginning of their journey, now guide them to the inner work ahead. Once they have taken the power of these symbols *into their own being* and have become transformed into perfected building blocks, they no longer need the use of the tools of their craft in tangible form and can rely solely on their inner guidance for infallible counsel.

§

IT IS TRUE that individuals could reach this state of inner illumination through their own efforts alone—but only with great difficulty and over an immeasurable span of time.

They need to absorb the light emanating from other "stones" that have already become luminous and, even more so, the light emanating from the monolithic columns that are to be found within the innermost of the Temple.

They must first do their *own* inner work—the work to which they have been guided by the symbols they have recognized within their being—or they will never be able to absorb the light that shines on them from all around. Thus it could happen that the master builders of the cathedral are forced to determine that here is a "dead" stone that must be removed from the Temple structure and be replaced with a different stone.

But if through inner work they progress to the point where the light that shines on them from all around can also illuminate their innermost being, their light will then shine forth for all Eternity and cast its radiance upon all future generations. Now at last they have arrived at the goal towards which they have been so arduously striving.

Those human spirits who once had fallen into the night of not knowing—those who have become incarnated into the darkness of this animal, physical existence—will be reunited with their own true Being. They will find themselves once again conscious of themselves as radiant, eternal beings, enveloped in the ocean of eternal Light.

❧

THE CATHEDRAL OF THE SPIRIT is not complete and shall not be complete until the last of the earthbound human spirits have found their way back to their home within the Light of Eternity.

In our day too, new workers and more stones are needed so that the construction of the cathedral may proceed apace.

All those willing to commit to the arduous task of transforming themselves into stones that can be used for the construction of the Temple will receive guidance and instruction from the realm of Spirit. They will learn to discover and decipher sacred symbols that will help them on their path—symbols different from the ancient ones stored in the lodges of today. These alternate symbols are needed because there are no longer people in the lodges who can interpret the ancient ones; thus, merely belonging to one of the lodges will no longer lead seekers to become skilled in the art of spiritual building.

Those spiritual aspirants, however, who are the designated custodians of the treasures of the old lodges should know that those symbols which they only honor out of a sense of piety and tradition, but without true understanding, contain the most profound spiritual wisdom. Indeed, with the help of the sacred symbols entrusted to them they might in time comprehend the deepest secret of the spiritual art of building, even if none of those they look to for counsel could ever reveal it to them.

But woe to those who are today's guardians of the implements and ancient symbols if they do not know how to preserve the sacred nature of the lodges. Woe to them if they no longer teach to build but instead teach to tear down what their great forebears once brought into being for the salvation of souls.

The wisdom of the oldest mysteries—the deepest knowledge of the Spirit which humanity had been able to attain and celebrate through the millennia—is preserved in veiled form in the lodges still extant today. Those who are unable to interpret what they have been given to guard should at least protect it from desecration.

❧

THE WORLD WILL ONE DAY witness once again the workings of those who truly know the Spirit's Truth. In time a body of wisdom will arise that will shine like a beacon of the Light of Eternity, amid the darkness and false lights of this earth.

At that time, however, many who today are allowed to approach the ancient mysteries without having been tested will be barred from gaining access to the sacred symbols—those symbols which have their origins in the realm of Spirit and which were created in the time of the forebears.

Rigorous testing will be needed in order to separate the wheat from the chaff. This is so that an atmosphere filled with the Light of Spirit, essential for work on the construction of the great Cathedral, can be created.

May those who in times to come earnestly aspire to find Truth discover once again what must first be fulfilled, so that the age-old practices that lead there can be revived.

May all who read this earnestly ask themselves whether they too ought not to pursue the sublime goal, held sacred through millennia—whether they too might not become workers and shape themselves into stones that can be used in the construction of the radiant, spiritual Temple of Humanity. In this noble pursuit, it does not matter whether they are members of a spiritual lodge or not.

Those who feel that they are able to undertake the work of transforming their being from a coarse, unformed stone into a stone that has been polished and shaped so that it can be used for the construction of the Temple of Humanity will find spiritual guidance from within. Such inner guidance will suffice even if no mentor from the outside world stands by their side.

The time has not yet arrived when *all* shall attain the spiritual insight that the ancient lodges—whose legacy is the venerable cathedrals of Christianity—once entrusted to their rigorously tested aspirants. But with a certainty ordained by the Spirit, those who have made themselves worthy in their hearts will again see the "blazing star" that stood above the manger, amidst the hapless animals of this earth, and the child through which the Light of Eternity returned once again to humankind.

❦

CHAPTER TEN

TRUE WORSHIP

T HE HUMAN SPIRIT HAS INVENTED COUNT-less ways to honor God over the millennia. Every human emotion has found its expression in these forms of worship, from highest spirituality down to the most barbaric coarseness, always reflecting the worshipers' own understanding of God.

The root of all these kinds of worship has been the belief in an anthropomorphic "God" who needs human beings to serve him—just as a lifeless idol needs human worship so as not to lose the only life it has: the life it has been given in the imagination and the subconscious of those who worship it.

To be sure, the more enlightened kinds of worship aim to uplift and stir the soul. Through sacred rituals and symbols, they may even tear open the deepest shafts within the worshiper, from which primordial feelings from the realm of Spirit may surface.

All this, however, is solely for the benefit of the *human being* and arises from the fact that the human spirit needs an external impetus to lift it up and needs these rituals in order to express its own relationship to the imagined, believed, or already perceived Ground of Being.

While enlightened worship can greatly stimulate human beings on their path to the Spirit's world, it is important to remember that such worship serves the development of one's own soul and does not, as is mistakenly claimed, serve God. This sort of worship is *not* what I mean when I refer to "true worship."

True worship is not service rendered to a deity nor is it a ritual celebrated as a way of paying tribute to God. It is, instead, the offering up of all one's energies and capabilities so that they may become servants of the divine Will: the voluntary submission of one's own will, without reservation, to the guidance of the Living God within—the core of the eternal spiritual within every human being.

It is release from the chaos of unruly desires; a process of crystallization in which every atom of an individual's energy freely subordinates itself to the cosmic, creative force and thus finds its proper place.

Human beings may seek to be uplifted by sacred ritual and the soul may be deeply moved by ritual magic, but a true union of the soul with the Godhead can only be attained by surrendering all one's energies to the divine.

This surrender is the one thing that can lead to the most sublime freedom. It teaches one how to become the master of oneself: to subordinate that which is lower in the self and align it with that which is highest in the self. In this way lower energies become attuned to the rhythm of the highest and "learn" to vibrate in harmony with them—and are thus preserved for all Eternity.

The wise person understands that the purpose of all true spiritual striving is precisely this: the harmonizing of all one's energies with the divine spark within so that one's consciousness can crystallize, in an ordered form, around that divine spark. As a result, individual consciousness can survive intact and be preserved beyond the death of the physical body.

Of what use are occult accomplishments, including the most incredible feats of fakirs, since they have only to do with the physical world? That world will vanish instantly with the death of the physical body, the moment the brain is no longer able to perform its role as a transformer of physical sensation into conscious awareness.

Of what use are clairvoyant gifts, since they only allow one to perceive the astral aura of this planet? True, this aura is invisible to most, and yet it is still only of this earth. Clairvoyants deceive themselves if they believe that what they see is close to the realms of radiant Spirit or even part of those worlds.

All intellectual insight, all knowledge *about* the worlds of Spirit, is of no use when every bit of it will disappear without a trace, like dust in the wind, to never more be found in the soul's consciousness—unless the soul's consciousness, while the brain still functions, is able to realize the timeless *will* to find union with its Living God, the divine spark of Spirit within its innermost.

❧

THE UNIFICATION within the innermost self of *all* the energies of the soul, of *all* the kinds of feelings and sensations that are possible including those that the physical body alone can perceive, is the one spiritual task that is truly worth every effort. This unification, however, can only take place within the innermost self, the soul's highest region of inner sensing and feeling—the only place from where the Godhead may be reached. It is within the innermost self that the Living God—the divine core of each individual—can be born, and only through the birth of the Living God within can human beings experience the Godhead.

"...the kingdom of heaven suffereth violence, and the violent take it by force." (Matthew 11:12 KJV)

One needs the "violent" force of will in order to free oneself from the distractions of the mind, to put away the intrusive thoughts and speculations that are concerned solely with the physical world, so that one may attain a state of inner quiet. In this inner quiet we may find the archetypal image of our own true self, which is our Living God: the indwelling God that in every moment of our existence creates us after its own image anew, and whose expression of timeless, ongoing creation we are. Our task is to bring ourselves into alignment with this divine source so that, out of the consciousness of our Living God, we may become able to preserve the consciousness of our own identity throughout Eternity.

❧

THIS FORCE must not be a strained exertion of will or an unnatural effort of concentration but, rather, a watchful, resolute rejection of every noisy urging of the intellect; a restraining of its presumptuous claim to speak with authority about a region that can never be accessible to it. It is this curbing of the intellect that alone makes possible "the great letting be"—the state that must be attained before the energies with which we sense and feel can become willing servants of the inner God from whom our being emanates. Only thus can the human being of Eternity within each of us be resurrected from its grave, newly born out of the Spirit—in the image and likeness of the "Father" who dwells in his "heaven."

The intellect can be used, however, to assist us in this striving—like a beast of burden that has been tamed to serve its master. We may also examine with the intellect what has been previously apprehended with the spiritual senses—to create an intellectual edifice, as it were, in which our spiritual experiences, like precious gems, may be stored. Indeed, without this self-created "treasury" our inner experiences, the jewels of our spiritual sensing, would be in danger of being scattered and lost in the whirlwind of everyday life.

But the intellect must never be allowed to take the lead when, by the first light of the dawning of insight, we embark on the path of the seeker—the path that leads to the indestructible core of life that is the center of every human being, our innermost true home, the unfathomable miracle within us all—"the jewel in the lotus flower."

The intellect is a good pathfinder when we set out on the path that leads to understanding those matters which impact the *physical* realm. Here the intellect may be fully trusted; it too is of divine origin and is a blessing when used wisely.

But if our desire is to reach God, we must not seek outside of ourselves—not even in that outer realm which most seekers mistakenly consider to be inner because it cannot normally be perceived with the physical senses.

Even if the human spirit seeks God within the highest regions of the Spirit's realm it will never in this way encounter God—just as the forces of nature cannot be found, as such, in the visible, physical world, even though their *effects* can be detected in every atom. The Godhead manifests itself only in the spiritual beings begotten by it and in each spiritual being differently according to its unique nature. God can never be found in isolation, apart from human beings, not even in one of the highest regions of the spiritual worlds.

We must discover God within our selves—as an eternal act of creation, eternally begetting *life*.

If we are to find God within, and not simply create an idol out of our own imagination—and thus fall victim to deception—we must trust the guidance of those who already are *alive* within God's consciousness; those who have surrendered their energies in service to the divine and who have united with the time-less archetype that begets them.

⚭

In this earthly realm, governed as it is by completely different laws, it would, of course, be foolish to expect to come across the highest spiritual beings in visible form. Human souls, even those who have already united with their living God and have mastered and consecrated all their energies to God, can never be free from earthly fetters as long as they are bound to a physical body. Even if they have attained the highest level of inner development possible for a human being, they may only reach the lowest level of union with the Spirit here on earth. Beyond this, those individuals who are united with their God and through whom a Mediator of Primordial Light has chosen to manifest here on earth would also be incapable of reaching the higher levels known to them through their own energies alone, without spiritual help from even higher beings.

To be sure, there are beings in the *spiritual* region of this planet who exist at a far higher level of perfection than would be accessible to them in a physical body here on earth.

They, however, have either long since been liberated of their mortal body or were never fettered to it because they did not succumb to the fall of the human spirit from its original home in the divine realm.

These high beings can only be felt *within* by human beings and, in accordance with timeless laws, can become visible and audible only to a soul completely united with God and then only under certain rare circumstances.

The few instances in which mortals, still bound by physical senses, were able to perceive one of these spiritual beings are extremely rare—but there have been countless reports of human beings who have fallen prey to deception and believed that a spiritual being had revealed itself to them through their physical senses.

∞

IT IS VIRTUALLY IMPOSSIBLE to eradicate the widespread delusion that clairvoyants are able to perceive these sublime spiritual beings. Thousands want to learn clairvoyance, thinking that they would then be able to perceive spiritual reality with their inner senses.

However, neither can one "learn" clairvoyance, nor have clairvoyants ever perceived anything other than the deceptive shapes and patterns and deceitful entities of a non-spiritual nature found in the astral—but by no means spiritual—aura of this earth.

Methods do indeed exist that can so over-stimulate the imagination of individuals such that everything they wish to see and hear will appear to them as real. Such deluded individuals may even gain "insights" whereby truth and delusion are grotesquely intertwined. They may perceive the grandiose visions created by their own fantasies, or those of others, as apparent reality. Yet who can doubt that such individuals are far more to be pitied than the real clairvoyants who are *born* with their questionable gift and who at least perceive something that is actually real within the physical realm—although they may mistakenly believe that they are beholding worlds of Spirit.

❧

THOSE WHO BELIEVE themselves to be striving towards the Spirit are deceiving themselves if they expect to encounter signs along the way that prove the existence of spiritual worlds in a manner that can be perceived by the physical senses.

Even if they were able to perceive all the worlds of radiant, living Spirit with their physical senses, this would not advance them one iota on their path; even if they were to engage in conversation with the highest spiritual beings over hundreds of years, they would remain at exactly the same level from where the conversation started.

Seekers should also not believe that, once death has freed them from their physical body, the whole spiritual world, with all its levels, will immediately be open to them.

In the Spirit's realm perceiver and that which is perceived must correspond to one another: beings can only recognize that which is of the same nature as themselves. Even spiritual beings who are united with their Living God can only penetrate to those levels that fall within their own level of spiritual attainment.

❧

WHENEVER NECESSARY, beings dwelling on higher spiritual levels will descend to lower levels in order to bring tidings of those matters of which they have knowledge. This is the case when a Luminary of Primordial Light unites with a mortal human being and thus becomes an embodied, Mediator of Primordial Light on earth. Higher spiritual beings may descend to lower levels for a time, whenever such a sacrifice becomes necessary, whereas beings at lower levels would destroy themselves were they to attempt—if such a thing were even possible— to penetrate to higher spiritual levels without the needed preparation. The strictest spiritual laws reign in all realms and that which truly is of the Spirit willingly obeys such laws.

The disembodied mental influences that every human being can experience do not stem from spiritual regions but, rather, from the lower realm of the unseen, physical world.

The timeless, primordial Light which illumines everything that is of the Spirit has wisely veiled its radiant rays so as to protect whatever is not united with Spirit, because its radiance can only be endured by that which is so united.

Of what use would it be to mortal human beings if they could gaze upon all the worlds of

Spirit as long as their *inner being* is not in absolute union with Spirit?

No hellish torments devised by the lower nature of human beings could be as cruel as the agony a human consciousness would have to suffer if it were able to behold the splendors of the Spirit's worlds before having united with Spirit and thus become able to share in the Spirit's life.

❦

ONLY ONE THING MATTERS: to willingly and without reservation offer up all our soul forces, all our bodily sensations, every impulse and every feeling to the Spirit—to the Living God within. Only in this way can the divine Spirit gradually unite with our human consciousness and then return to us these forces, senses, impulses and feelings as willing servants, once we are prepared to master them, guided by the timeless, radiant core that continually gives birth to our Being anew.

This is the inner state of true worship that all seekers must achieve if they wish to take their mortal consciousness with them to the life beyond, not just for vast stretches of time but *for all Eternity.*

"I must work the works of him that sent me, while it is day: the night cometh, when no man can work." (John 9:4 KJV)

Here in this life on earth it is possible for us to work—to continue to develop. After the physical world has been left behind, souls will find themselves in the condition they created for themselves while on earth, and in which they must now passively remain. They must wait until, without their own doing and, to use earthly terms, only after millennia—or, for those who have advanced further on their path, perhaps a shorter period of time—their souls have been purified to the degree that it becomes possible for those spiritual beings who are already united with their God to awaken within them a consciousness of the divine core of their being—their Living God. Only then can that turning of the will occur through which all their energies can be surrendered as servants of the Living God. Only then can the union of their consciousness with the timeless consciousness of divine Spirit be accomplished.

By the time these souls have been united with their Living God, their earthly, human consciousness will have long vanished, like a forgotten dream.

There is no act of "grace" by the Godhead that can help them hasten or circumvent this fate.

Even though they have been "saved"—united with the Living God within them in the life beyond—their life on earth with all its strivings, joys and hardships, will forever be beyond recall. They have not achieved the ultimate victory: the expansion of consciousness that is the prize of those who have worked towards union with their Living God *while still on this earth*—the outermost realm in which the divine expresses itself.

They, too, will nevertheless one day become an expression of the divine Spirit and shall be united with their corresponding masculine or feminine polar opposite to live in the boundless bliss of life within the realm of radiant Spirit. Yet, their experience of self will not equal that of those who, along with the limitless happiness that is now theirs, are still able to experience the consciousness they had when they had descended to the lowest depths and were united with the human animal and incarnated in a physical body.

Just as the awe experienced by those who live in the flat landscape of the plains as they behold the majesty of mountains can hardly be understood by those whose entire lives have been spent in the mountains, only those spirits who have retained the memory of the profound depths they once traversed can appreciate the full measure of their present bliss. Thus, the higher they ascend, even if it should take eons to reach the highest levels, the less would these souls want to be without the possibility of remembering the lowest level to which they had descended.

❧

NOTHING THAT IS OF THE SPIRIT can ever be changed in its essential nature; so too, the soul's divine core—which is at every moment begetting the soul—never changes as it ascends to higher spheres.

The Living God that dwells within the human being's innermost—the divine core with which one's consciousness may unite already here on earth—remains the *same* at every spiritual level that may be attained throughout all Eternity.

It is the *state of consciousness* of the soul that expands in order to attain ever higher levels of spiritual consciousness and thus become able to sense the ever widening, infinite dimensions of spiritual being.

If it were only a matter of the individual attaining *any* level of consciousness within the soul as the soul forms itself around its ever-begetting spiritual core, then every effort to unite one's consciousness with the Spirit during life on earth would be superfluous. This union can, in accordance with the eternal laws inherent in the Spirit's life, still be brought about in the life beyond, even if only after eons. The only exception is where there has been a complete dissolution of an individual's consciousness.

Every authentic spiritual teacher in every age has called upon humanity to awaken *while still here on earth* because at stake is the highest possible happiness of the soul throughout Eternity—the soul's ability to preserve its earthly consciousness and with it the ability to remember its sojourn on earth. Beyond even this, the unspeakable agony a soul may suffer once it has left the mortal body can be avoided if the soul is able to unite with the Spirit during life on earth.

This is the task of those out of whose midst I offer my teachings: to lead humanity in every age, through those who are called to speak Truth, onto the pathway that can lead to increased happiness. Every word of this book has no other purpose but to teach this kind of true worship.

May none who read these words depart from this life of toil and tribulation before their consciousness has been united with their Living God.

May none ever find themselves in that night in which it is impossible to develop and rise through one's own efforts—the night from which there is no escape until the unredeemed soul's debt has been paid down to the last farthing.

Now it is still day and helpful hands are at work, ready to offer spiritual help to all who ask for it. No esoteric teaching or "guru" is needed to receive such help.

"He that hath ears to hear, let him hear." (Matthew 11:15 KJV)

❧

REMINDER

"Yet here I must point out again that if one would derive the fullest benefit from studying the books I wrote to show the way into the Spirit, one has to read them in the original; even if this should require learning German.

"Translations can at best provide assistance in helping readers gradually perceive, even through the spirit of a different language, what I convey with the resources of my mother tongue."

From "Answers to Everyone" (1933), *Gleanings*. Bern: Kobersche Verlagsbuchhandlung, 1990

For a deeper understanding
of the core of Bô Yin Râ's teachings
you may want to read:

The Book on the Living God,
The Book on Life Beyond and
The Book on Human Nature

These three books should be
read together.

A description of all three books follows.

The Book on the Living God

The Book on the Living God describes the inner path that leads to birth of the Living God within—what we must do and what to avoid on the long journey towards awakening the consciousness of our timeless self.

Ordinary consciousness, Bô Yin Râ tells us, is actually like sleep; there is a greater consciousness that is alive in us, informing every cell, and our task is to unite it with our self-awareness.

We must also set aside the ideas we have been taught about an anthropomorphic God. God is not meant to be an external object of worship but, rather, an experience to be awakened within us. We are cautioned to avoid the pitfalls that might divert us: following false teachers or believing that certain foods or exercises, or ecstatic experiences, have spiritual merit. Everyday life, when lived with attention to the ultimate goal, will lead us towards a gradual awakening of our timeless self.

E.W.S. Publisher

Contents: Word of Guidance. "The Tabernacle of God is with Men." The White Lodge. Meta-Physical Experiences. The Inner Journey. The En-Sof. On Seeking God. On Leading an Active Life. On "Holy Men" and "Sinners." The Hidden Side of Nature. The Secret Temple. Karma. War and Peace. The Unity among Religions. The Will to Find Eternal Light. The Human Being's Higher Faculties of Knowing. On Death. On the Spirit's Radiant Substance. The Path toward Perfection. On Everlasting Life. The Spirit's Light Dwells in the East. Faith, Talismans, and Images of God. The Inner Force in Words. A Call from Himavat. Giving Thanks. Epilogue.

The Book on Life Beyond

The Book on Life Beyond is a guide to help readers understand what they can expect to find in the life beyond death, and how to best prepare for it.

Bô Yin Râ explains that life beyond is actually another dimension of the same life we know here on earth—just as real and solid, but perceived through spiritual, rather than our limited, physical senses. He emphasizes the direct connection between our actions here on earth and their effects on life beyond. We bring with us into life beyond the same state of inner being with which we departed, and are able to experience its wonders exactly to the degree to which we have developed our spiritual self. For example, those who have failed to show compassion for others and have lived selfishly will find that life beyond lacks the warmth and light that other, more developed souls can perceive.

Bô Yin Râ counsels us to mentally practice the "art of dying" as a meditative practice to prepare for the transition from physical to spiritual existence. The goal is to constantly orient one's thinking, emotions and desires toward transformation of the self, in order to be able to receive the spiritual help that will be available to us after death.

E.W.S. Publisher

Contents: Introduction. The Art of Dying. The Temple of Eternity and the World of Spirit. The Only Absolute Reality. What Should One Do?

The Book on Human Nature

The Book on Human Nature presents basic concepts about human nature with the goal of inspiring readers to awaken the timeless, spiritual spark within. We become fully human only when the spiritual potential within us gradually awakens and infuses our material, purely animal selves. It is a path that every human being may and should pursue.

A central understanding is that all life results from the joining of opposites, in particular, the polarity of male and female energies. Bô Yin Râ emphasizes that the true spiritual human being is male and female united in one entity; when we seek our spiritual self, we must call forth the male and female in ourselves and in all things. He discusses the biblical fall from grace as a descent from the spiritual plane, in which male and female were united, onto a material plane, in which male and female are split apart.

Bô Yin Râ warns men that holding onto the illusion of male superiority means forfeiting their spiritual life. While the spiritual paths that are natural for men and women are different in tone—open and receptive for women, active and grasping for men—they are equal and complementary. He tells us that *true* marriage is preparation for the life beyond: by coordinating the desires, wills and attitudes of two beings we once again bring about, in some measure, the original state in which male and female energies are united.

E.W.S. Publisher

Contents: Introduction. The Mystery Enshrouding Male and Female. The Path of the Female. The Path of the Male. Marriage. Children. The Human Being of the Age to Come. Epilogue. A Final Word.

THE KOBER
PRESS

www.ingramcontent.com/pod-product-compliance
Lightning Source LLC
Chambersburg PA
CBHW022121080426
42734CB00006B/208